P9-BUH-631

Excellence

2006 Poetry Collection

Copyright © 2006 by The America Library of Poetry
as a compilation

Copyright to individual poems
belongs to the authors

All rights reserved

No part of this book
may be reproduced in any way
without the expressed written permission
of the publisher

Published by
The America Library of Poetry
P.O. Box 978
Houlton, ME 04730
Website: www.libraryofpoetry.com
Email: generalinquiries@libraryofpoetry.com

Printed in the United States of America

THE AMERICA
LIBRARY OF POETRY

ISBN 0-9773662-1-9

Contents

Poetry by Division

Excellence

... In memory of Kendall Wathen and Zach Tracy

Blizzard
by Kendall Wathen

My rabbit Blizzard is fluffy and white
She is very active but she still sleeps at night
She lies down in her cage
On all sunny days
My fingers in the cage are like a lure
They attract her chin with her soft fur

Count On Me
by Zach Tracy

Soccer is the sport I play
I'm the keeper, and I'm here to stay
I stand alone in the goal
Hoping like heck to save my soul
I try my best as I stand there tall
My nerves are raw
As I wait and watch
I hope a lot I won't get squashed
I always do my best out there
As a keeper, I am rare
I never let my teammates down
If I do, I wear a frown
I now play select
But I still miss the rec.
I hope I continue to learn
To catch the ball and hold it firm
For my teammates, count on me
I won't let them down, you wait and see

Foreword

There are two kinds of writers in the world.
There are those who write from experience, and those who write from imagination.
The experienced, offer words that are a reflection of their lives.
The triumphs they have enjoyed, the heartaches they have endured;
all the things that have made them who they are,
they graciously share with us, as a way of sharing themselves,
and in doing so, give us, as readers, someone to whom we may relate,
as well as fresh new perspectives
on what may be our common circumstances in life.
From the imaginative, come all the wonderful things we have yet to experience;
from sights unseen, to sounds unheard.
They encourage us to explore the limitless possibilities of our dreams and fantasies,
and aid us in escaping, if only temporarily,
the confines of reality and the rules of society.
To each, we owe a debt of gratitude;
and rightfully so, as each provides a service of equal importance.
Yet, without the other, neither can be truly beneficial.
For instance, one may succeed in accumulating a lifetime of experience,
only to consider it all to have been predictable and unfulfilling,
if denied the chance to chase a dream or two along the way.
Just as those whose imaginations run away with them, never to return,
may find, that without solid footing in the real world, life in fantasyland is empty.
As you now embark, dear reader,
upon your journey through these words to remember,
you are about to be treated to both heartfelt tales of experience,
and captivating adventures of imagination.
It is our pleasure to present them for your enjoyment.
To our many authors,
who so proudly represent the two kinds of writers in the world,
we dedicate this book, and offer our sincere thanks;
for now, possibly more than ever,
the world needs you both.

Paul Wilson Charles

Editor

Editor's Choice Award

The Editor's Choice Award is presented to the author
who, more than any other, in our opinion,
demonstrates not only the solid fundamentals of creative writing,
but also the ability to illicit an emotional response
or provide a thought provoking body of work
in a manner which is both clear and concise.

You will find "So Clean and So Young"
by Emily Mergel
on page 201 of "Excellence"

Spirit of Education
For Outstanding Participation

2006

Allen Ellender
Middle School
Marrero, Louisiana

*Presented to participating students and faculty
in recognition of your commitment to literary excellence.*

Division I
Grades 3-5

I'm Unlucky
by Darnell Ross

I am very unlucky
I broke my toy ducky
My favorite basketball popped
My mother's vase dropped
Then everybody blamed it on me
How unlucky can I be?
I got gum in my hair
My butt stuck to the chair
I lost my pet bunny
Everybody thinks it's funny
Why did this happen to me
How unlucky can I be?
When I rode my bike I fell off
My landing was not soft
Then I broke my arm
My hand got tangled up in yarn
Now can you see?
How unlucky can I be?

Kit-Kat
by Josie Linell

Green window, white wall
Little kitten waiting for night to fall
Her black shiny fur, her jingling collar
Her round nose and pointy ears
Her eyes full of exhaustion starting to close
Good night, Kit-Kat

Monkey In a Jungle
by Brinley Macnamara

In a jungle, there was a monkey
He loved to eat bananas but then he got real chunky
His mother said to stop eating those bananas
But he did not stop, so she had to call his nana
He ate and ate and ate, until he got real big
Then he got real sick, from then on he ate a fig
This teaches you a lesson, not to eat so much
Like this monkey did or else your stomach and head will touch

Trees
by Tiger Henderson

It's summer now, and leaves are found
Upon the trees of Cindor Town
Summer's getting cold, soon it will be fall
Leaving colors of orange and red, and soon no leaves at all
After fall comes winter, leaving trees cold and bare
Walking along the trees alone, would give you quite a scare
Soon after that cold harsh winter, comes warm and sunny spring
Trees regain their leaves, and bluebirds come to sing
Don't take life for granted, notice all the leaves
Always smell the flowers and always see the trees

Blue
by Amanda Beaudoin

Blue sky, up high, wavy blue ocean, too
Gloomy faces feeling sad in blue stained glass windows
That's why I wear my blue fleece
My blue glasses on my eyes to see Pluto in the sky
My poetry folder that I'm writing with
The blue chairs we sit on everyday at school
Blue tubs against the wall containing all our work
My blue math binder in my tub ready for math class
School is out, time for a little snack
Of blue raspberry slush, a blue lollypop too
Makes my mouth turn very blue
I drive past gardens with blue flowers
I pass blue houses, blue cars too
I ask myself, "Is everything blue?"

Fish
by Cooper Sodano

Different colors, different kinds
Some can see good, some are blind
They live in the ocean
They swim with motion
They have gills to breathe
They don't have fleas

Bio Poem
by Paul Garcia

Paul
Friendly, funny, athletic, shy
Brother of Isaiah, Andre, Victoria
Lover of sports, pizza, and chocolate
Who feels joyful when I make good grades, nervous on the first day of school
And mad when I make poor scores
Who needs a dog, to watch less TV, and practice his recorder
Who gives gifts to family and friends, food to the ducks, and hugs to his family
Who fears heights, snakes, and being lost
Who would like to be a police officer, learn how to skate
And travel around the world
Resident of Kentucky
Garcia

Up At the Plate
by Benjamin Browning

I walk up to the plate with sweat running down my face
I am always nervous!
I smell the delicious aroma of hot dogs coming from behind the dugout
I see the pitcher winding up, the ball fires from the pitcher's hand
I am ready, my feet are lined up straight
My knees are bent, my hips face the pitcher
My hands are securely wrapped around the bat; my eyes are on the ball
The ball flies toward the plate
Smack!
The ball goes as far as Mars!
I feel fantastic! I hit a home run!

Emerald Green
by Tyler Forbes

Emerald green is grass that had morning dew
Emerald green is the peacefulness of a town when everyone is asleep
Emerald green is the "Happiness award" given when I win chess tournaments
Mint chocolate chip ice cream on a summer's day at the park is emerald green
Emerald green is the color of my girlfriend's eyes that look at me with joy
Red, yellow, and orange, but the best of all is emerald green

The Civil War
by Millie Cahoon

The Civil War was a crazy thing
Fight, kill, fight, kill, bombs go bang
Confederates or Union, who will win?
All this is mostly about whether slavery should end
Union disagrees, Confederates do not
So to settle this, they fought
Even though the war was mad
Fighting again family was sad
Many events such as the March to the Sea
Union killing every Southerner they see
War is finally over, Union had won
So now today slavery has gone
Yes, yes, slaves are free
Now their faces are filled with glee
Now you know about the Civil War
The war of victory, the big war galore

Heaven Above
by Bethany West

Heaven is like love and kindness
On a bright sleek cloud in the bright blue sky
Angels all around and you can do whatever you want!
Where wishes and dreams never end!

Summer Days
by McKenzie Vaught

Summer days are blue and bright and really shiny half past night
Summer flowers are here and there, but summer animals are everywhere!
Summer days ... count them daily for they're quite lovely
Come again and lay thy head down as winter begins
Summer days are quite a special moment worth waiting for
For truly summer is coming
Peek your head out dear summer and peek your head back in
For winter is not just a long cold day away
So peek back in summer and go to sleep
Get really warm and rest for summer days are almost over
Celebrate them because tomorrow is the beginning of fall!
Summer days are almost over!
We love summer days!

My Old School
by Dion Hodson

My old school is a zoo
I hate my old school, lunch killed me
Our class was way too small!
My gym partner was a monkey
My teacher got fired and was replaced!
The principal was mean too
The gym teacher was tough, too tough
Then I moved, finally

The Moon
by Anjali Vishwanath

The moon was once only a big piece of the sky 10,000 years ago
And now she turns her beautiful face upon this world below
Her forehead is a shining blond, her cheek as hard as stone
Her eyes are the bluest eyes that I have ever known
The moon shines her bright glow in the cold dark night
Beautiful moon; her eyes so pretty, she is a wonderful sight
If you look in the sky but not at noon
You will see bright stars and a fantastic glowing moon

Football, Until We Die!
by Terrelle Wood

Football, football! Can you catch it?
Run, run! Hey, boy, go fetch it
Make the touchdowns all night and day
Sleep seven hours, wake back up and play
Throw, throw! Can you throw it?
Run, run! I'm going to catch it, you know it
White thread, brown skin
When can you come down, when, when, when?
Come down, come down, can you see it anymore?
Zoom, zoom, it hit the floor
Good game, good game! Who won it?
Too bad, too bad! We lost it
Next time, I will zoom like a fly
We will play and play until we die!

Christmas
by Vahe Balagyozyan

I love sledding
I love Christmas
I love snow
I love December
Santa is my best friend
I love snow, Santa, and school
I love when Santa gives me toys or shirts

Sleep Is ...
by Chris Cefole

Sleep is relaxing; sleep is quiet
Sleep is comfort; sleep is joyful
Sleep is warm; sleep is lying on the clouds
Sleep is your own world

Winter
by Briley Graves

It is winter
I taste hot chocolate on a cold, snowy day
Peppermint candy canes as they hang from the Christmas tree
And pumpkin pie with whipped cream in Mama's kitchen
It is winter
I feel the cold, white snow freezing on my hands
Christmas ornaments sticking me as I hang them on the Christmas tree
And snowballs hitting me in the face in a snowball fight in my backyard
It is winter
I hear the ripping of the Christmas packages on Christmas morning
Christmas carols being sung by my family at church
And Christmas bells ringing all through the cold day and brisk night
It is winter
I see glistening, white snow falling outside my bedroom window
Little kids making fat, fluffy snowmen after the first winter snow
And all of the pretty Christmas decorations hung throughout the town
It is winter
I smell spicy, hot chili simmering in my sister's kitchen
Rich, chocolate pies baking in the oven at Granny's house
And the wood from the fireplace as it snaps, crackles, and pops

I'll Be Glad
by Shelby Watts

Don't wake up in the morning, when you haven't said your prayers at night
The next night when you go to bed, the moon won't seem as bright
If I could go back in the past
I'd make it fun while it could last
It would mean everything to me
I mustn't carry the problem on my back; it doesn't make sense to me
If I can't do what I want to do, it won't be as bad
But I'll still be as sad
So when you hear that bird's song with its little rhyme
You will be happy that you had enough time

Mary
by Monica Olson

Kind, normal woman
Married to a carpenter
Gave birth to Jesus

Summer
by Chase Dodson

It is summer
I see fuzzy, grey squirrels climbing trees looking for food
Red cardinal birds flying high up in the sky
And children running and jumping as they play outdoors
It is summer
I hear birds chirping loudly first thing in the morning
Cars roaring and crashing into one another at the demo derbies
And my parents cheering loudly when I'm playing baseball
It is summer
I taste cheesy, broccoli casserole homemade by my mama
Salty, crispy potato chips served at our family cook-outs
And garden fresh strawberries with lots of sugar on them
It is summer
I smell roasted barbeque hot dogs rolling off the grill
The burnt smell of firecrackers on the fourth of July
And tires burning rubber at the demo derbies I attend
It is summer
I feel the cold, refreshing water as I jump into the swimming pool
The gritty sand between my toes while I play at the beach
And the hot, pouring sun when I ride my four-wheeler

Soccer
by Taylor Rondeau

Let's make a goal
Just don't let it roll
Run up and down the field
After your leg has healed
The soccer ball is white and black
I am sure it will not crack
When I kick the soccer ball
I feel strong and tall
If you think soccer is the best sport ever
Then you are definitely clever
I am going to play soccer with my friend
I will tell you what the score is at the end

Family
by Darrikk Kitts

My family is very special
I'll do my family count down
First of all my dad, he can be grumpy
But that's because he gets kind of slumpy
Now my mother is very nice and is as pretty as can be
Although she says it's hard for her to see what I can see
Next comes Tara, you don't want to meet her
Because she's the wicked witch of the west and I can't beat her for sure
After that comes Donnie, he's not very nice
He'll trick you like he tricked me, into giving him the money for the spice
Last comes Preslee, she's the last one
She doesn't like to have any fun
So that's my family count down
And now you know what's so special

What I Found
by Donnie Groot

Guess what I found in my desk and locker
I found a TV in my desk
I found spider men in my locker
My sister found homework from one month ago in my desk
I found a monkey and Tad in my desk
I found my homework from three years ago in my desk
I found my dog in my desk

Wind Poetry
by Macey Klosterman

There's nothing like a gentle breeze
Blowing through the limbs and leaves
I love to feel it on my face
It gives me such a sweet embrace
The feeling rushing through my hair
The feeling of the flowing air
You can never see it there
But it is, without a care
Wind can also be so strong
Twisters can make things go wrong
It can rumble, roar, or ring
Twisters lift most anything
Wind can blow straight up or down
It blows across or all around
Or it can be most quiet and calm
With winds like that, there's no alarm
Wind can be a friend or foe
Its speed can be so fast, or slow
Wind poetry can be so soft
It's like a bird that flies aloft

Diving At the Beach
by Halle Conway

Diving in the ocean so deep
Maybe more than one hundred feet deep
Taste the salt on my tongue
Feel the sand at the bottom
Dive in as a dolphin and come out as me
It's so much fun to swim under the sea
Feel the rush of the waves coming near
Are those seagulls I hear?
See them go in the water and dive
Hoping the fish are there and alive
Swimming with my hands looking like prunes
Look over and see the huge sand dunes
I love diving in the ocean; it's so much fun
Come and join me everyone!

Dreams
by Sarah Schlueter

Dreams are a burning summer day
Dreams are anything you choose
You are making dreams by expressing yourself at night during your sleep
Your dreams can be scary or happy depending on what you saw before bed
Dreams are showing you something you've never seen
You're having your fun in a dream doing something you may never do
You will always have a dream
Dreams are a burning summer day

My Mother
by Emma Wang

A kind soul to me
Loving, caring, forgiving
A soul I can trust

A Poem For Spring
by Katelyn Brown

Spring is a beautiful season
When flowers grow and bees swarm
The birds will tweet
Boys and girls will go out to play all through the day
Hip-Hip-Hooray, Hip-Hip-Hooray
We are out of school today!

The Knight
by Connor Legare

Once upon a time there was a knight
On a sparkly brown horse
The knight has a spear to attack the enemy that trespasses
He will scare or even kill them with his spear
The knight was supposed to guard a castle
That had a king and queen inside
Then one night there was a witch
That cast a spell on the knight
And he turned into a frog

Comical Canine
by Konner Grossman

Mia, my Chihuahua, is as funny as can be
She's really smart, and as small as a rat
Whenever we're eating, Mia bounces from spot to spot around the table
Begging for food with eyes wide open as big as golf balls
Her mouth wide open with her tongue sticking out
Straight forward to catch any drop of food
As soon as she notices even the tiniest piece of food about to fall on the floor
She sprints toward it, catching it in midair
Whenever we're playing, I would throw her toy rabbit towards her
As soon as it hits the ground, she pounces on it
Pinning it to the ground with razor sharp claws
Believing it's prey for her, then she starts chewing it like it is food
Whenever we're outside, when she sees a dog ten times her size
She stands still, puffs up as if she is bigger than that dog
Then she starts barking angrily, showing off her tiny, but sharp teeth
That is what I call a funny little dog!

Spring Flowers
by Lakisha Haynes

Spring flowers are pretty and so are you
If I were them, I would smell like perfume
You never know what you might see
Except a bumblebee in the spring
Like a tree is tall and you bounce a ball

Loneliness
by Hannah Lembright

I am a grain of sand left on the beach
I sit there all alone
Staring into the lone plain I lay along
I would love to be blown away by the wind
Onto other beaches with my friends
As I sit there all alone, thinking of how to play
On this warm, bright, sunny day
A sudden gust of wind blows me along until I fall to the ground
What I land on is a mystery
I hope for it not to be a horrible land of more sorrow, isolation, misery
Loneliness is like one grain of sand left on the beach

Kids
by John Steven Mays

Kids
Spelling words, solving open responses
Making textile designs in art class
Using dictionaries to help with homework
Studying dinosaurs that are extinct
While younger students sound out vowels
Solving math and science problems

Pride
by Mellyssa DeOliveira

We take pride every day
In living in the U.S.A.
But what is it that makes us love our country so much?
Is it the purity on a soldier's face?
Or is it the flag's majestic grace?
Is it the peoples' kindness, so tender and true?
Or is it the losses, so few?
Or is it just because it's our home?
The place where I'm meant to be
The place for you and me

Todd
by Jacqueline Mills

Look at me, my eyes as blue as clear water dripping down a stream
My hair like streaks of sun waiting to soar in the sky
My lips as red as an apple waiting to grow up and bloom
My nose a potato, with holes drilled inside
And my fingers like long, grown carrots

Grandma
by Abby Hoagland

Grandma
Nice, yellow hair
Runs as fast as cheetahs
Happy always with pretty eyes
Grandma

Summer
by Mary Brook Anderson

It is summer
I see a lot of hot swimmers as they dive into the pool
Sweaty, determined golfers when they are playing eighteen holes
And sparkly, shining fireworks being shot on the Fourth of July
It is summer
I hear loud, booming fireworks as we shoot them off the boat
The splashing of boys and girls when they dive into the pool
And the loud barking of my dogs after the coyotes arrive
It is summer
I taste yummy, fresh watermelon right off the watermelon vine
Great, sweet lemonade, fresh-squeezed by my mama
And hot, spicy barbeque on a nice, summer day
It is summer
I smell the sweet roses growing in Mama's flower garden
Smoky, hot barbeque coming from Dad's grill
And the yucky, nasty water as I dive into Dale Hollow Lake
It is summer
I feel the soft petals as I pick Mama's roses
The long, sweaty fur of my dog's coat
And long, shaggy, brown hair when I pet the horse's mane

The Promised Land
by Kayley Bryson

Feelin' hungry all the time, master's not giving momma enough food
Having to be whipped to git up, having lashes on my back
Wanting to go to a free place, where no one is forced to work
Momma and Poppa talked low and we do not want to be whipped
We will leave tonight; we crawled
Havin' chicken pox is no fun, does not feel good
But we crawl into a safe house
We face master shooting and bloodhounds howlin'
Something fierce trying to sleep, but can't
Having to run or will not be free
The bears are fierce, scary and threatening
Hoping the master does not shoot!
Just then, a young girl, her sister, her momma, and her poppa
Walked out and took us in, she gave us food and water
We jump up and down and sing! We are so happy to be free!
Feelin' great because we made it to Canada! But can goin' back still make us free?

A Very Strange Duck
by Patrick Lally

There once was a duck from Hungary
Every day he filled his tummy
But whenever he ate
He tried to eat the plate
That very strange duck from Hungary
That very strange duck from Hungary
When he went to see his mummy
He said to her, "Quack!"
And he got a big smack
That very strange duck from Hungary
That very strange duck is back again
This time he's looking for a hen
He found a chicken
Who made him sicken
Every single bird in the den

If I Were a Shark
by Zachary Whiles

If I were a shark, I would hear
Waves splashing and crashing with a huge splash
"Brooommm," of the motorboats as they go by
People screaming because they see another shark
If I were a shark, I would see
Fish that swish to get away and the bottoms of the boats as they go across the water
Finally, I would hear screaming and shouting
Of people, because there are sharks nearby
If I were a shark, I would smell
Blood drifting through the water, dead fish in the sea
Dead, rotten meat people dump from boats
If I were a shark, I would feel
Water when I go up and it splashes me
The sea, and I would feel seaweed hit me in the face
If I were a shark, I would taste
Bones crunching in my teeth, meat getting stuck in my teeth
Finally, I would taste salt in my mouth
If I were a shark, I would realize
I would have a hard job to do, and I would have to swim a lot
Last but not least, I would need to eat a lot

The Black Fox
by Stanley Dang

I saw a black fox
That lived in a box
It had small paws
And a lot of claws
It had slick, smooth fur
And a really sweet purr
It had a fluffy tail
And it was as gentle as a snail
It had a small nose
That was as cute as a rose
I saw a black fox
That lived in a box

Rain
by Allison Daniels

As the rain falls it makes some sad
Others glad, and many disappointed
As the rain falls it washes the street clean
Makes soil soggy, and plants healthy
As the rain falls it makes some happy
Some sad, and many disappointed
As for me, I'm in the middle

The Dreams You Can Catch
by Lily Wilding

The dreams you can catch can be a red-horned devil
Or a perfect princess dream that is right at your level
With your beautiful, sparkly dream catcher
You can dream of a fluffy, big, ugly animal, named the fenatcher
"You lucky duck," I say to some people that have caught the perfect dream!
Some dreams are perfect, like you being free
Although some dreams are bad, and they send a horrible bad-dream flee
If you clean your dream catcher every night, you'll be clear of all night frights
Also, if you clean it every night, you will get dreams of hope, peace, and happiness
So before you go to bed, read this poem
And clean your dream catcher and hope for a perfect dream

Coming To America
by Hope Wilding

We're finally here in this big place
There's sweat dripping from my face
I can't find my way around
It's like everything is upside down
At last we find a home
It looks like a small dome
Everyone in my house shares a room
We don't eat breakfast until noon
Our dinner is fish and chips
My clothes are full of holes and rips
The children call us hurtful names
We don't participate in fun and games
I go to work everyday
At home I never get my way
We go to bed at eight o'clock
On our door, we never hear a knock
I always do my best
Like a mother bird building a nest
This country isn't such a mystery anymore
But now at least we're not poor

Playful Haggis
by Darcy Simpson

Playful Haggis loves to play tug-o-war
Tugging on a rope, with his strong teeth pulling me off the couch
Making me fall on the ground with a big thump
And let me tell you, it hurts
It's like he is stronger than eight oxen pulling together
His big glassy eyes bulging out, staring straight at me that he is the winner
Playful Haggis loves to play circus
Standing on his hind legs he shakes my hand with his huge 2-pound paw
He grins with a long side face that tells me he wants to do it again
Playful Haggis loves to play roller-skate
With my roller-skates on, I hold onto his leash
As he sprints in front like a jaguar
Wagging his tail side-to-side, slobber flying everywhere as he pants
Taking on the lead, never wanting to go home
Time to get a drink, Haggis looking down at the surface of the water
Glittering like a thousand mirrors
"Slurp, slurp", "woof, woof!"

Zookeeper
by Taylor Tranthem

If I were a zookeeper, I would hear
Children laughing, "Haha!"
Monkeys going like this, "Ooohh!"
Lions growling, "Rahhh!"
If I were a zookeeper, I would see
Monkeys swinging from tree to tree
Children laughing at the monkeys
Giraffes standing tall as a mountain
If I were a zookeeper, I would smell
Cotton candy scent as children eat it
Stinky odors of an elephant's habitat
Aroma of buttery popcorn as it pops
If I were a zookeeper, I would feel
Fluffy hair that feels like cotton when I pet the lion's mane
Cool water as I wash my hands
Fuzzy, stuffed animals as I sell them to the children
If I were a zookeeper, I would taste
Yummy popcorn on my break
Cold, fizzy soda as it goes down my throat
Flavorful, cotton candy as I eat it
If I were a zookeeper, I would realize I could tame lions
I would hear children laughing
I would see monkeys swinging from tree to tree

Brady and Chip
by Kristen Corbett

They have eyes that are brown
Ears that are pointy, little button noses and are as happy as two clowns
They love to share bones, taking walks together
And running on the beach in all kinds of weather
When they listen and obey, they are rewarded with a treat
Sometimes too many, then they have no room to eat
When nighttime falls, it's time to rest
Only the boys get the very best
All cozy and warm in their queen size bed
They float off to dreamland with memories of their day tucked away in their heads
They say a dog is a man's best friend
I agree and know they will be with me until the very end

Jazz Dance
by Mary Crosby

I love to dance, all kinds of dances
But my favorite of all is jazz
When I am dancing jazz, I feel like I am in my own jazzy world
Twirling and like I am being carried away in a tornado
My body curving in different directions
Leaping forward, leaping backward, as the music blares from the stereo
I love to dance, all kinds of dances
But my favorite of all is jazz
Feeling unstoppable, thinking about the next step
Stretching out my limbs like a swan in motion
My heart thumps fast with the rhythm of my steps
I love to dance, all kinds of dances
But my favorite of all is jazz
Dancing on stage, the audience cheering, standing on their feet
Clapping loudly, calling out my name as I get off stage
I love to dance jazz!

Summer
by Aubrey Thompson

It is summer, and I smell gas from the jet ski as we fool around in the water
The cocoa butter scented beach towel as I dry off and hang it on the side of the boat
The spicy, hot barbeque, steaks and hot dogs sizzling on the grill
As Cory does all the cooking
It is summer, and I see people relaxing under the trees on the grassy banks
People splashing in the water near the shore at the lake's edge
Having fun with their families
And lots of children swimming in the water around the boat dock
In their colorful swimsuits
It is summer, and I taste delicious chips and dip that I savor while lying in the sun
Icy cold Dr. Pepper from a bottle in the cooler as soon as I get off the jet ski
And soft, tangy oranges that my brother and I gobble up
At the table inside the houseboat
It is summer, and I hear deafening fireworks piercing the stillness of the night
The motorboats and jet skis speeding across the water as people shout happily
And lots of children screaming as they splash and scamper in the vast, deep water
It is summer, and I stumble on a razor-sharp in the shallows near the bank
The soft, slimy seaweed squishing between my toes as I wade to the shore
The blistering sand of the beach scorching my feet as I search for a dry towel

Senses of Fall Coming To Life
by Makena Devlin

Oh, fall, oh, fall, oh, fall, I love you
Oh, fall, oh, fall, you're the best of all
The crinkle of the leaves when I spring on top of them
Autumn leaves crunching beneath my feet
Chicken sizzling over the grill, the fire crackling noisily
Sweet, hot cider on my tongue
Candy being popped into my mouth
And tasting like sweet, sour, and mouthwatering flavors
Chilly and soft breeze, blowing against my face
The first flakes of snow, drifting into my mouth
Smoke rising from the chimney
Delicious Thanksgiving dinner, fantastic hot mashed potatoes
Oh, fall, oh, fall, oh, fall, I love you
Oh, fall, oh, fall, you're the best of all

The Sky
by Helvert Martinez

Mighty, wonderful sky
I wish I could fly
Days and night forever

If I Were a Pediatrician
by Marissa Keith

If I were a pediatrician, I would hear, "Wah, wah!" crying babies
Nurses talking to the baby's mom and dad
Friends speaking to grandma and grandpa
If I were a pediatrician, I would see baby's mom and dad, sons or daughters
People looking at their babies
If I were a pediatrician, I would feel excited to be going to work and seeing kids
Tired after I got off of work
Great because I would be there for them
If I were a pediatrician, I would taste eggs for breakfast
I would drink coffee and eat my lunch, too
If I were a pediatrician, I would realize I would have to be gentle with babies
Careful with other kids so I don't give them the wrong medicines
My job is important because I get to take care of kids

The Jealousy of the Flea
by Emily Farrer

One day a flea met a fly
When they were flying by
The flea, you see was quite aghast!
To see a bug fly by so fast
"Oh, his secret I must know!"
Cried the flea all aglow
And so he spied upon that fly
As his jealousy grew, but then he got quite angry!
As the fly teased Spider McBlue
"And now it's time to show that fly what I can really do!"
Cried the flea as she flew straight towards McBlue
Snap! Bite! So don't let jealousy go to your head

School
by Michaela Rowe

Homework, fun, cool
Listen, teacher, student
Work, recess, gym, art
Computers, reading
These are things I do at school

Cape Cod
by Jessica Linnell

Cape Cod, a wonderful place
When you are there, it won't be a disgrace
The cape full of cod
Everyone's happy, like peas in a pod
Falmouth, Mashpee, Orleans, Brewster and Harwich
Yarmouth, Dennis, Barnstable and Sandwich
Truro, Wellfleet, Provincetown, Eastham
Friday night, a band in Chatham
Play it soft in the winter
Play it wild and crazy in summer
They catch our fish with bait
Making seafood that's really great
Fish and shells
And you can tell
With salty air
Cape Cod is very fair

Tennis
by Emma Harney

"Gulp" goes the water down the nervous athlete's throat before the game
It is time, time to shine
They slowly walk up to the court
At the baseline they are given a small green tennis ball
If that one important green ball does not go
In the two upper squares, a fowl will be called
"And it's in," goes the intimidating reporter
Back comes the rebound; the opponent hits a lob, back it is hit!
And the score is 15- love, ten minutes pass; they call a break, now it is 15- all
The sweaty athlete takes another drink
With a few encouraging words from the coach and they're back on
After the final score of the game is 50-30, they win
Happy faces fill the air; they threw the tennis ball up without a care
If you come to the court with an open mind, you leave the court a champion

When I Play Baseball
by Cameron Correia

When I come to bat
I give the ball a splat
I run all the bases
Ignoring all the faces
I see the ball go to the glove
As the fans cheer above

Watermelon
by Kristina Baker

I love to eat watermelon
They do not have skeletons
They're juicy and sweet
And they are good to eat
I spit out their black seeds
Because those are things I do not need
The light of green lines on the dark green shell
Remind me of jail cells
They are not great for picnics
Anyone can eat them, even St. Nick
They're bought by the pound
You can eat them all year round

Bluey and Archey
by Sally Chinn

Bluey and Archey make me feel safe during thunderstorms
My stuffed cat and my blanket, from when I was a baby
Bluey and Archey make me feel safe during thunderstorms
Bluey wrapped around me, Archey in my hand
Bluey and Archey make me feel safe during thunderstorms
Bluey is as soft as a cloud, I hear Archey's nose cracking
When I grab him during thunderstorms
Bluey and Archey make me feel safe during thunderstorms
I can feel my fingers getting stuck in the holes of Bluey
Grasping it when I am scared, I feel the hole in Archey's arm
Bluey and Archey make me feel safe during thunderstorms
I can see the blue and white squares on Bluey, I can see Archey's stiff tail
Bluey and Archey make me feel safe during thunderstorms
Bluey and Archey!

Deep Sleep
by Justin Kennady

Deep sleep that comes to pass
It creeps up behind you and whispers, "It's time to go"
With every person it persuades
Tackling, slamming, crunching your heart
It's a deep sleep like a cave swallowing the light
So don't give in, for it shall cut your life thin

Racing
by Beatty Duncan

I love my racing bike
A gift from my parents on Christmas Day, the best surprise ever
Now I can race on the dirt bike track, going down the giant smooth hill
Hitting the huge ramp at the bottom, zooming past other riders
Fighting for first place, pedaling as hard as I can
Sweat dripping down my face, drowning me
Making my clothes stick like glue on my body
As I squeeze past other races to the last turn
I pump my bike, pulling up and pushing down on my handlebars
To keep my speed up, going over the small bumpy bumps
Flying to the finish line, coming in first place
I love my racing bike!

My Mom Is a Super Mom
by Randall D. Hatcher

My mom is a super mom
She can handle two active boys of her own
When she wants us to stop and listen, she screams out at the top of her lungs
Furiously, as if she's about to explode, immediately we stop and listen to her
She knows how to get our attention
My mom is a super mom, she is very strong
When my brother and I get right in each other's faces
She gets right in front of us and stretches her arms out
And separates us away from each other, she knows how to separate us
My mom is a super mom; she always wants us to tell the truth
Whenever we argue, she will send us to separate rooms
Giving us the time to cool down our steam
Before calling us to hear our side of the story
She knows how to calm us down; my mom is a super mom
She is the best mom in the world

The Bat Cat
by Katherine Dutile

What's that shadow I see at night?
I can kind of see the color, it looks bright white
It makes me jump, it breathes in air
I think it's an animal because it has hair
I look around, it's still in sight
I look at the switch, should I turn on the light?
I flip the switch and look at that
The whole time I was afraid, it was only my cat

The Hawk
by Jacob Lowell

I hear the screaming cry
As the brown figure soars over me
It cries as it plunges toward the lake
Splash!
It has a fish!
It cries once more
Then it soars away

Spring Day
by Madeline Farrer

Bright new blossoms sitting high in a tree
Gently blows the wind, as careful as can be
Glorious sun rays beat down all in a haze
Nothing I can say is more beautiful than this spring day

The Monkey
by Jimmy Cochran

I wish I were a monkey
In the Franklin Park Zoo
I'd play all day and sleep all night
And then perform for you

Math
by Molly McIntyre

Math is very confusing and very hard
It's as bad as anything, and as boring as a birthday card
With all those numbers and all those signs
While everyone slumbers, they'll wish they were Einstein
But, as hard as math may seem, and though it makes you sleepy
Someday you'll want to scream that you know math, even if it's creepy!

Love
by Griff Weber

Sick in bed with your eyes closed, just laying there
Your skin all wrinkly and pale, laying there for weeks unable to talk
But you can hear me telling you how my day was and how much I love you
A smile on your face, telling me that you hear me, making me feel happy
Sick in bed with your eyes closed just laying there
I miss us playing chess together, even though you always won
I miss playing golf with no score
I miss going to Bellarmine basketball games with you
I prayed that you would get better, so we could have good times again
But sometimes you looked better, but you were only getting worse
But now you're gone forever, your eyes never to open again
Quietly I talk to you when I'm feeling down
Hoping that you hear me to help me feel better
Papa, Papa I love you so

I Am a Dog
by Chris Sesco

I am a dog
You know me for running
My mother is a dog
I was born in my dog house
I live in a dog house
My best friend is a bat
Because he hides, we like to play football
My enemy is another dog
Because I am a dog
I fear you
Because you might hurt me
I love me
Because I'm fun
I dream (or wish) I lived inside my master's house

Dreamer
by Brittney Boucher

I lay my head on the pillow, as I say my night time prayers
Soon my eyes will close and I won't be in despair
Far away in dreamland I dream of all my thoughts
And all the bad dreams, my dream catcher caught
In the morning when I wake
I'll always have my dreams to take
So when you're down and feeling blue
Think of your dream, it will come to you

The Pencil Stealer
by Nolan Flaherty

I used to love to use it, I used it everyday
I loved that mechanical pencil, but now it's gone away
My mechanical pencil was the best
I used it for homework, I used it for tests
My mechanical pencil was unique
That's why it was stolen by some geek
If you are the one who took this item, please give it back!
So future fifth grade assignments I can happily attack!

My Number One Sister
by Daniela Reuter

Talks to me when I need to talk to somebody
Helps me when I am scared, lets me sleep in her bed
Not like any other sister, bugs me all the time
Long, light brown hair, never makes a mistake
Plays sports with me, tall, straight up high
Takes care of me, wears makeup
Thirteen years old, annoying, number one sister

Popsicles
by Amelia Gonyea

Popsicles are my favorite treat
They are really fun to eat
All the colors glow
All the colors of the rainbow
Flavors, flavors explode in my mouth
When I talk about popsicles I am a blabbermouth
My favorite color is blue, which is cotton candy
I love it, just dandy
The other colors are okay, too
But I like cotton candy, boo hoo
Pink, orange, purple, or blue
What's your favorite, I have no clue

The Winning Hit
by Jared Snyder

It was the championship football game
All the players were nervous
Some were shaking with fear of losing
Others with churning stomachs about to throw up
I tried not to think of it to avoid being distracted
One minute left on the clock before the end of the game
Our team ahead by one point, too close to celebrate
I was as scared as a mouse running from a cat, afraid to lose the game
I shot across the line of scrimmage, dove to the left, boom!
I tackled the quarterback who fell down holding the ball tight
I jumped up and down screaming, "We won! We won!"
All around me were players high-fiving me with excitement

Colors of the Rainbow
by Haley Partin

Colors of the rainbow are all around
If you don't believe me look near
There are seven, count yourself
Roy G. Biv
Red, orange, yellow, green
Blue, indigo, and violet
See the colors of the rainbow are all over
And on you too!

Mushu
by Austin Scheibmeir

Mushu, my betta, is dead
Lying under the filter
Sucked in by its powerful pressure
Its eyes gently closed as if sleeping peacefully, never to open again
Its body floating like a boat in a lake
But stuck in one spot as if glued to death, never to move again
The light in his cage shining dimly on it
Drawing attention to its death in its darkest moment, never to see the light again
A rush of sadness fills my body as I flush him down the toilet, "Kerplunk!"
It swirls and twirls before finally disappearing, never to be seen again

Pie
by Marvin Labbe

I love the smell of pie,
Well, I walk by it, it catches my eye
I love the flavor banana
And the person who makes, it is my nana
I love that sweet tasty treat
The taste is magnificent and can't be beat
I love that sweet delicious smell
'Cause when I smell it, it rings my bell
I love that crunchy crust
It makes me want to go nuts
You get to the cream
It tastes so good, it's like you're in a dream

My Teacher Is a Duck
by Lindsey Young

My teacher is kinda weird
I don't know what to do
My whole class cheered
Well, she certainly isn't you
Well, maybe I should tell you
I wanted to pick and pluck
I don't know what to do
My teacher is a duck!

If I Were an Apple
by Morgan Witt

If I were an apple I would hear
Branches snapping, tractor motors and birds chirping
If I were an apple I would see
Farmers picking apples below me and crates full of apples
If I were an apple I would smell
The smoke of tractors, girls' perfume and the fresh air
If I were an apple I would taste
The sweet apple juice, water from the sky and a slice of apple
If I were an apple I would realize
I'm the only living apple, I taste good and I'm healthy for humans

Family of Five
by Colin Dean

My dad works every day
Even with three of us, he still comes out to play
My mom does the laundry, also the dishes
Even though she's so busy, she grants us all our wishes
My brother Alex, he's not so bright
Even though he's twelve, he sleeps with a night-light
Then there is my last brother Brady
Even at age nine he acts like Slim-Shady
So that leaves me, I'm in the middle of three
Which is good for me
A loving family of five
I'm lucky to be alive!

The Traveling Star
by Sarah Brady

As the star sits alone, a burst of energy strikes
The star gets its power and takes off
Past Pluto with its freezing cold air
The star ready to give up light, the star keeps moving
Next to Neptune, still very cold
The little star finds a way to emerge, and moves on
Bursting past Uranus, so cold, moving so fast, almost past this planet
Next to Saturn, the little star's favorite planet
Beside the famous rings, sadly now leaving
Beside Jupiter, the largest planet in our solar system
Feeling very small, and now leaving
Next to Mars, better known as the red planet
So very vivid, the little star still moves on
Right near Earth where life lives, as he leaves the observers, still moves on
Next to Venus, the second planet from the sun, so hot and yet still moving
Next to Mercury, so close to the sun
The little star is still moving, finally at the sun I shine so bright for the world to see

Springtime, Springtime
by Rebekah Kennedy

Springtime, springtime, flowers bloom
Birds sing to me and you
Everyone will fly their kites
And we will see some pretty sights
Springtime, springtime, time to play
Kids will play and play all day
Children will be out of school
And that is really, really cool
It is time to go and swim
And sometimes you'll get caught on a limb
Hip-hip hooray, hip-hip hooray
We are out of school today
Now spring is ending, and summer is near
We will get to play outside, have no fear
Storms will quickly come and go
And we will get to see the ocean flow
It is time to go to a beach
And swim, and swim until we can't reach

No More Slavery
by Kyle Martens

Feeling upset because I do not get food
I feel sad, lonely, and hungry because my family has been separated
Wanting to touch Canada's soft, free land
I want to eat free food
Decided when blisters on my hand
Calluses on my feet and slashes on my back from my master
It takes me through the woods with chilling air down my spine
We crawl through bushes to Canada
Facing howling hounds, my master with a deadly gun
We hide in the bushes, hoping they go away
It makes me feel terrified; my heart feels like it's coming out of my chest
Help! Is that a house with a lantern shining in the window?
A shelter from the chilling air and my master
Acting free when I get to Canada, I dance, cry for joy
Feeling excited, happy, but sad because I lost my family

I Want To See a Place Or Two
by Halle Conway and Gabriella Weithofer

I want to see a place or two
But I especially want to see them with you
Like the Grand Canyon so high
It could almost reach the stars in the sky
Or the bottom of the ocean so deep
It might go over a thousand feet
I want to see a place or two
But I especially want to see them with you

Buzzing City
by Jessica Lee

When the city turns on everything buzzes
Horns honk, engines roar
Footsteps pound from store to store
Yells of voices, screeches of brakes
Makes the city louder
Night and day, it never turns off
Until the exhaustion comes
And puts it away

Follow My Heart
by Fernando Gonzalez

The sight of good old T-Kweng
My mom coming home from work
Spending a day on the beach
It all makes me happy
The sight of a basketball game
A tennis match with my aunt Irma
The start of football season
It all makes me happy
The view of the lake while we are fishing

National Disaster
by Arianna Robichaud

National disasters are plain disasters
Jenny sits on the stoop of her house
As the downpour came stronger on a summer night
Her dad was lost to a flood
She sat thinking hard
Her hands pruned and her clothes soaked
She squeezed her hair and a million drops came out in a million milliseconds
She was thinking national disasters are plain disasters
She just can't help thinking it when the rain comes
But she carries on, walks inside with her dad in her heart once again

Seasons
by David Deng

Rainy, dreary, blooming
Beautiful flowers are anywhere
April showers will bring the beautiful spring
Sunny, sweaty, air conditioning
Ice cream is a real treat
4th of July will begin the splendid summer
Windy, chilly, falling leaves
Foliage can be quite a sight
Thanksgiving will end the colorful autumn
Snowy, weary, snow shoveling
Skiing may have a lot of fun
Christmas will warm up the white winter

Summary
by Chelsea Spears

It is summer
I see lawnmower tracks left behind by Pa's lawnmower
Gold, sparkling fireworks on the Fourth of July
And a beautiful wrapped present for my daddy on his birthday
It is summer
I hear hummingbirds singing as they approach the bird feeder
My dogs, Brisket and Max, bark when they see the moonlight
And the crumbling of wrapping paper while Dad opens his gifts
It is summer
I taste rich dirt pudding made especially for me
Salty, red tomatoes straight from the garden
And hot, spicy chicken coming from the barbeque grill
It is summer
I smell stinky fly spray to help repel the flies
The strong smell of bleach in the chlorine inside the pool
And the aroma of smoke coming from the grilled steaks
It is summer
I feel the bumpy road while riding the four-wheeler
My dog's smooth fur coat as I pet on his back
And the cool, refreshing water when I get thrown into the pool

Books
by Tava Hoag

I really love to read books
When I pick one up I'm hooked
Books can be scary, funny, sad
No book can make me mad
I can read in the morning and noon
I can even read by the light of the moon
I can read when it rains or snows
When my sister comes in I say, "Go, go, go"
When I read a book in the park
My dogs both start to bark
When I go to sleep I think about books I've read
And I try to make one up in my head

Dance
by Amanda Michienzi

Feeling happy when you dance!
Jump, spin, leap, turn
Shoes, pink, black, tan, hard, soft, loud
Gold at nationals with all my friends
Jump, spin, leap, turn
Lights on, music starts, dance, music stops, cheering
Gold at nationals with all my friends
Being free when you dance
Lights on, music starts, dance, music stops, cheering
Hard work always pays off
Being free when you dance
What is your favorite way to dance?
Hard work always pays off
Shoes, pink, black, tan, hard, soft, loud
What is your favorite way to dance?
Feeling happy when you dance!

If I Were a NASCAR Driver
by Kevin Neal

If I were a NASCAR driver I would hear
The "vroom, vroom" as cars blow by me
"Vroom" as I blow by other cars
Boom! As cars crash and blow up
If I were a NASCAR driver I would see
Other cars trying to pass me, smoke as cars tear up
Oil on the track as it leaks out of other cars
If I were a NASCAR driver I would smell
Oil the other cars lose, smoke from my tires when I take off
Gas from other cars
If I were a NASCAR driver I would feel
My engine blow up, a flat tire, my car spin as I wreck
If I were a NASCAR driver I would taste
Dirt as I wreck in the grass, smoke as my engine blows up
Dust as another car wrecks
If I was a NASCAR driver I would realize
My family would depend on me; I could win my first championship
I could make enough money for my whole family

My Bad Dream
by Ashley von Borstel

I woke up one morning as sad as I could be
I had a bad dream, and it was about me
I was drifting in the sea, and I was all alone
I couldn't see land, and I couldn't go home
The sea was stormy, the water was gray
I could feel the coldness; it was a very dark day
I lay in my bed, glad that I was now awake
I had an enormous adventure, but it was more than I could take!

Snowy Day
by Stephen Bedrosian

It was a really snowy Friday, walking to school
It was a really snowy school; no recess should mean no school
It was a miserable walk home, I felt blind, all I saw was white, white, white
Thank God we are home
We had good hot chocolate
When it started to clear up, I slightly put my face out the door
My face started to shiver
When it cleared up I finally went outside
I shoveled a path in the deep, deep snow

The Stamp Act
by Karli Lauyans

The Stamp Act is a fact
One more step to being free
Though it didn't fill us with glee
It angered us
So we made a fuss
"No taxation without representation," they cried
Some who stood up to Parliament may have died
Some were accused of treason
Without any reason
They decided to boycott
Which was the way they fought
They made a petition
To beat their competition
When they won, they were free
And they were truly filled with glee

Welcome Back
by Mariah Tyree

I hope you enjoyed your trip to France
Did you do fun things, like laugh and dance?
I tried to imagine the things you would do
Like go to fancy restaurants and eat tasty food
I missed you a bunch, and that's a fact
So I wrote this poem to say, "Welcome back"

Bundle of Joy
by Brian Condon

My bear is my bundle of joy
I've had him since I was two
I hold him when I have the flu
He's old and torn under the right arm
I still love his sweet, little charm
My bear is my bundle of joy

Birds
by Rafael Silva

Mother birds nesting in the trees
I wonder if she likes fleas
Birds flying and singing in the sky
It makes me want some cherry pie

Martial Arts
by Andrew Brandt

Martial arts is close to my heart
It is a fine art
We never wear shoes or socks
It's kind of like learning to box
Mr. Cody is my instructor
He is just like a conductor
He wants us to concentrate
I can feel my heart rate
If I get really good
I will be able to break wood
I like my white uniform
My last class was during a storm

Bad Choices
by Mary Nedderman

Crash
Is the headline of the newspaper
Someone wrecked again
A wreck from a drunk driver
I don't understand why people drink!
"I miss him," someone says
I am at a funeral
My uncle had passed away
I don't understand why people die
My dad lost a friend the other day
The man smoked
He died from lung cancer
I don't understand why people smoke
But I do understand that choices can lead to death

Hangman
by Emily Smith

The word! The word!
What can it be?
Confused like crazy, but still guessing
I have half the body, and half way through the alphabet and still nothing
What can it be?
I've got three letters, down to the last guess,
I got it! Oh, that's it!
The word is word!

Night
by Francesca Korte

The moonlight shines on my sleeping face
And stars dance around the sky, so merrily and peacefully
The darkened seashore is quiet and still
Besides the soft crashing noise of the waves
That will tomorrow splash on my face
The streetlights' eerie glow shines upon the cold, undisturbed streets
That usually guide the way to somewhere, but not now
The dream I am dreaming is like the peaceful, dancing stars
Until morning comes and brightens the world, and turns night to day

Madness Is a Tidal Wave
by Nathan Tippenhauer

Madness is a tidal wave, maybe sometimes loud
My madness is very long; the stirring problems are when people annoy me
My yelling is the high waters rising, my frustration is things being broken
The waves are a destructive hit, when my fist punches the brick wall
Strong winds are physical violence, used when nothing goes my way

Playful Dad
by Sanjana Satish

Curly, dark, black hair
Sparking eyes
Thinking like me
Wonderful
Pleasing voice
Smart like me
Gives lots of hugs
Gives lots of kisses

Diver Dave
by Timothy Mills

There once was a diver named Dave
Who fell into a cave
He tripped on a rag
His head fell in a bag
Ever since, he's been locked in that cave

One Black Day
by Francesca Boyatt

One black day I saw black clouds
Moving over the sky covering up the sun
I got worried
Lightning shook a tree
Black clouds hitting each other
Boom!
I ran like a tiger, my heart was thumping
Bam! I slammed the door- safe

Gymnastics
by Katie Towne

I love to do gymnastics, it's so fantastic
I did it for two years, without any fears
My coach was very nice, I did the bars twice
We practice in a gym, and I never broke a limb
We had to wear uniforms and they keep us warm
We do not wear shoes, so we don't lose

Butterflies
by Myrria Lyncee

Butterflies, butterflies flying so high
Way up high in the sky
They fly free
As you can see
I cry when they leave me
But still I could see
That they love me
And I love them
Fly little butterflies
Fly free-free-free
Just for me, only me

Winter
by Jacob Shirley

It is winter and I taste snow cream that my mother makes
The warm hot chocolate from my kitchen when I come inside
And hot homemade soup just off the stove, on a cold winter day
It is winter and I feel the icy cold snow as it hits my face
The Christmas tree boughs all sharp and prickly when I touch them
And the beautiful ornaments that are smooth and hard, as I put them on the tree
It is winter and I hear laughter in my house as my family gathers
The rattling of paper as we unwrap presents on Christmas morning
And bells ringing outside as carolers sing, outside, in the falling snow
It is winter and I see snowflakes falling softly and covering the ground
Children playing in the snow with their thick coats and warm mittens
Happy people sledding down snowy white hills, on fast sleds
It is winter and I smell creamy hot chocolate heating in my kitchen
Ham and sweet potatoes baking in the oven on Christmas Day
And smoke from the fireplace in the living room, as we watch football

The Clock
by Mihaela Manea

Tick tock
Goes the clock
Tick tock
A minute passes
An hour passes
Then a day
Tick tock
Goes the clock
Tick tock
A week passes
A month passes
Then a year
Tick tock
An endless clock
Tick tock, tick tock

Sheep In a Red Jeep
by Connor Horn

Sheep, they like to ride in a red Jeep
Sheep, they don't make a peep
"Man," said the sheep, "what a cheap Jeep"
"Where shall we keep the key to this cheap Jeep?" asked one sheep
Another said, "A garage is needed for this cheap Jeep"
"A mouse has stolen our cheap Jeep, wrecked it, and left it in a heap"
The sheep tried to fix the Jeep
However, the sheep didn't know how to fix a Jeep

Barehanded Catch
by Brian Smith

Water splashing in my face, bouncing on the waves
I am going light speed behind a motorboat
Soaring like the eagle
Swish, swish, splash, going side to side
I put my hand in the water, it is cold and brisk
I stand up, I feel like a king
I look back down, I see colorful fish
I try to catch one; I fall out of my tube
The water is bitter; I am frozen, but I catch my fish

Winter
by Kayla Murray

It is winter, and I taste icy snow
As it cascades out of the sky, onto my waiting tongue
Chili and peanut butter with crackers in my Granny's kitchen
When my sister and I spend the night
Sweet candy canes that I like to swipe from our festive Christmas tree
It is winter, and I feel my wooly coat snug, keeping me toasty
When I go outside to play and make stacks of snowballs to bomb my sister
And my warm, toasty blanket that keeps me warm and comfy
On long, drawn out winter nights
It is winter, and I hear bells on Christmas Eve from my grandma's church
Snow trucks plowing, scraping the snow off the roads
For the cars and trucks to get through
And the rustle of wrapping paper
As we assault our presents early Christmas morning
It is winter, and I see children building snowmen
To stand sentinel in their front yards
Lighthearted people ice skating upon the frozen ponds
Gliding gracefully with windblown faces
And laughing children lying flat on the frozen ground
Making angels in the snow
It is winter, and I smell logs smoldering in the fireplace that keeps us snug
Hot chocolate waiting for me
Bubbling on the blazing stove in my mother's cozy kitchen
And sizzling, buttery popcorn as we keep an eye out for Santa
Late on Christmas Eve night

Clothes
by Else-Marie Nelson

This morning when I woke up, I looked for what to wear
When I saw my closet was a mess, I wore a distant stare
So many things were on the floor, I couldn't count them all
I felt like my clothes were very big, and I was very small
When I finally found my shoes, I worked my way to the door
I almost screamed, I almost blew, I couldn't take it anymore!
My room was a mess
I was covered in stress
I didn't know what to wear
I thought to myself just maybe, I should rip out my hair
So today when I went to school, I wore a shirt that's red
Then my brother said to me, that's what you wore to bed

Grandpa
by Tayte Bullinger

I love him
Now the light is very dim
Because he is gone forever
He inspires me
I wish he could come back, gee!
I would be so grateful if that happened
God is the only one who can make him come back
He was like a tack
Because he always stuck to what he was doing until it was done
I wish you could come back!

Hope
by Blake Herbert

I hear the rushing water
The sand is soft
But it can't steal my troubles
I can't believe this
It is tearing me apart
The sky is full of stars
And dolphins flying in the sea
And I remember
Dolphins are beautiful like the stars at night
Yet dolphins and stars die
Just ... like ... hope

Friendship Never Ends
by Tiani Paula

Friendship never ends
Why? Because friends are a lot of fun
You can depend on fun
Fun, fun, run, laugh, play, and learn
Never have to wait your turn
Fun friends are friends that can make dreams come true
They can even cook you brand new food
Friends can help you along the way
And say to you, "What do you want to do today?"
They're the ones that you can trust when you're feeling blue
Guess what? Best friend, "I love you"

Darkness of Night
by Emily McEvoy

I look out my window and what do I see?
I see the velvety black of night
I see the stars winking from up above
Sparkling and shining for all to enjoy
I see the moon not yet whole, hidden a little by the clouds of rain
It glows and illuminates the darkness of night

Fall
by Holly Ford

It is fall
I see the colorful leaves as they fall to the ground
Children trick-or-treating on Halloween night
And the nice neighbors handing out candy to the kids
It is fall
I hear leaves rattling as we rake our yard
Birds chirping loudly when they nestle in their nests
And the wind whistling and blowing on a cool fall day
It is fall
I taste creamy pumpkin pie with lots of Cool-Whip on top
Warm, moist turkey at Granny's on Thanksgiving Day
And golden delicious apples after they fall from the apple tree
It is fall
I smell giblet gravy when Granny cooks on Thanksgiving
The turkey roasting in the oven inside Grandmother's kitchen
And buttery rolls as I set them on the dinner table
It is fall
I feel itchy leaves as I jump in a leaf pile
The cool fall air when I go outside to go to school
And the warm Thanksgiving meal as I eat at my family's house

Under the World
by Faith Siebert

Last Tuesday when I was under the world, I was tired and wanted to go home
Last Tuesday when I was under the world, I was sad and lonely
Last Tuesday when I was under the world, I wanted it to be Wednesday in a hurry
Last Tuesday when I was under the world, I felt my eyes getting tired
Last Tuesday when I was under the world, I opened my eyes a crack
I looked at the calendar, it was Wednesday!

Meow-Meow's View
by Emily Esten

I see a batch of cat food, sitting in a black dish
A cup of whitish water is beside it jiggling
The gray tile floor, boring to see, hate to look at it
Light gray infant, crawling towards me
Enormous grin on the itsy-bitsy face
Infant throws cat food at me
Showers over my head like cat and dog rain
Huge person, moves gray infant
Infant has foggy tears falling down
Move back to food, more gross than ever
Lumpy and old, it's blucky mold
Huge person returns, hurrah!
Gives clear water to me, yummy black-gray food
Waterfall landing in my empty pool, bowl becomes full
Only five minutes in the colorless life of me
Meow-Meow's life!

Science
by Katie Harris

Science is so confusing
It makes my brain explode!
And makes me feel like
My lovely head ...
Got run over in the road

Flower Bud
by Olaf Eide

It's been sitting there for hours
I've been watching it all day
That great, big, giant flower bud
I don't know what to say ...
Wait ... it's coming open now
I see a little color
It isn't just a flower
It's something the bees just might devour!
I'll go and show it to the world
But should I give it to a girl ...
No way!
Not in a million years

Ladybug, Ladybug, Fly Away Home
by Maranda St. Martin

Ladybug, ladybug, fly away home
Where you will roam, roam, roam
Fly, fly away
To where you can be free and play
Ladybug, ladybug, fly away home
With your red back and polka dots
And clear, shiny wings
Fly where you can be free
Ladybug, ladybug, fly away home
Landing on a flower, enjoying your time
Be careful if there are frogs
You might hear a sudden crunch
And find out that you are his lunch
Ladybug, ladybug, fly away home

Swish
by Evan Allen

Double cross-over, then drive, no, look past to the shooter
The little jumper from the baseline, "Swish!"
Get back on D, get the steal, take it to the hoop, "Swish!"
Down by two with four seconds left, get the ball in and wait till the last second
I take the three pointer, "Swish!"
Jump up and down, scream till I die, then it plays back in my mind
"Swish," but it was only a video game

Tubing
by Joseph Bannon

When you go you have to sign in
To get a weird pass and a tube
Now you are ready to go
Get a hook, and go up the hill
Excited, scared, fearless
Now you are getting ready to go down the ramps
You are going so fast
You're so excited
Now you are trying the big ramps
You are going even faster
"It is really fun, I love it!"

Death By Day
by Jordan Marie Jackson

Something happened, so terrible, I can't even explain
It's my mamaw, that's what I called her, she died at the hospital
Went into a deep sleep never to awaken, never, death by day
At the funeral, many people came, staring, some weeping
Waiting to say the last goodbye, death by day
Memories of Mamaw, knitting, fine, and beautiful
Wearing simple jewelry, giving big bear hugs, death by day
- In memory of Lois Jackson, December 2004

What Am I?
by Christopher Preece

I am a desk
You know me for holding stuff
My mother is a tree, my father is a couch
I was born in a workshop, I live in a classroom
My best friend is a pencil, because we help humans; we like to work
My enemies are kids because they will write on me
I fear fire because it will burn me
I love paper, because I like holding it
I wish I were a human

Nature
by Alex MacMillan

Nature is so beautiful
How I wish I could be a sunflower
I would respect the birds and the bees
I would be open all day and close at night
The birds would eat my seed
They would have to save some for the winter to eat
The bees will get nectar from me
They will bring it to their homes
My nectar will be their food for the winter
Nature is so beautiful
How I wish I could be a sunflower
I would respect the birds and the bees

The Rich Cat
by Maddy Fougere

Once there was a rich kitten, and some tough alley cats
The kitten was mean and snobby, can you imagine that?
He was selfish and greedy, he wouldn't share at all
And when the alley cats walked by, the kitten climbed the wall
One day the kitten lost his wealth, that greedy, snobby kitty
He asked the alley cats for food, but they would have no pity
The story's lesson is not to be selfish, and you will find it will pay
If you help your friends, they will help you some day

Friendship
by Desta Pickering

If you have a lot of friends
You should play outside till the day ends
You can play basketball or soccer
Until the day gets hotter
Friendship should last
Even if the good times should pass

Pooky
by Lejla Setka

Pooky's delightful, but howls with fright
Sometimes I wish he'd be out of sight
He's soft and cuddly because of his hair
Sometimes I wish he's a bear

Boy Named Joe
by Matthew Murphy

There once was a boy named Joe who is lucky to be alive
He stole his parents' car and took it for a drive
He's in the hospital now with a few broken bones
His parents are still with him, but he continues to moan
His parents are quite mad, but they are grateful that their son is okay
Joe feels so sad because he hurt a man playing croquet
This story tells you to never steal your parents' car
Because you will regret what might happen and you won't get very far

The Best Teacher, Mrs. Lawson!
by Landon Corolla

I got a teacher that sits on the bleachers
No homework because the teacher is sick
The aide has to watch us so now we can have a parade
So flip on the desk, and get some tips
Oh no! The teacher is back
Well, we had a good week when we had six-packs
Time out, teacher was back
Our aide had a backpack

Halloween
by Ian Huschle

Halloween
Great, fun
Trick-or-treating, eating, walking
Getting lots of candy
Jack-o-lanterns

The Guinea Pig Food Pyramid
by Jenna Fossum

Carrots, apples, celery, hay
Our favorite is dandelions in May
The food we get is so delicious
It's what we call guinea-pig-nutritious
We eat with a crunch and a munch
Totally enjoying our healthy lunch
"No, we would not like to eat pellets today!"
We would much rather just run away
Screaming, "Yeek!" gets us a better treat
Lettuce and spinach, we eat and eat
We always save the best for last
And then we try to eat the rest fast
We hide the good stuff, even from best friends
Till they find it, then the game ends
We friends bite each other till we can't anymore
Then we eat our food quickly till our mouths are sore
While fighting, we scream and cry and whine
Finally our owners give us the gift divine
Dandelions, hung from twine!

Dragons
by Michael Metz

Dragons are majestic creatures, along with their riders
A dragon soars through the air, blue scales glimmering
Black saddle, a black blur as the dragon soars through the air
The dragon loops, the rider slowly falls
The dragon dives to catch him, he lands on his graceful dragon
Swoosh, the dragon zooms downward
The dragon smoothly lands on soft grass; there is another dragon
With shimmering gold scales like little gold lights in the moonlight
In the early morning, they ride their dragons from dawn until dusk

The Biggest Lake, In All Creation
by Rachel Hoskins

The biggest lake in all creation
Is where I spent my vacation
A large body of water in the heart of Dixie
I went tubing with my Mimi
Skimming quickly atop the lake
Losing my grip was my mistake
I flew up in the air scared out of my wits
Then crashed into the water, it nearly broke me to bits
The lesson is clear I hasten to note
If you value your health, then stay on the boat

I Love
by Malik Carr

I love kickball
Kicking high, higher than a bird can fly
Launching it high in the sky so people can't catch it
As I zoom to the first base
I love to play kickball
Watching for the roller to roll to the next kicker
As I get ready to dash to the next base
I love to play kickball
Rushing through third like a bull to hit home base
As my friends cheer me on shouting, "Go Malik, go!"
Making me feel as happy as a baby bird that just learned to fly
I love to play kickball!

Storm!
by Sarah Green

Drip, drop, drip, drop
Rain falling from above
Sky no longer blue, ugly gray color of sadness
Boom! Thunder
Sister runs to my room; scared of sound we hide
Under bundles of covers
Streaks of light come in windows
Lightning makes no sound
Lights that light the sky
Not asleep any more
Drip, drop, boom!
Lights make a storm
Could be scary, could not
It's a storm, a storm
Storms here, storms here
It's pouring cats and dogs
Bright lights come again
Then storm is done, storm is done

I Am Water
by Shania Mollette

I am water
You know me for quenching your thirst
My mother is a river in the woods
My father is an ocean near the beach
I was born in a creek
I live in an ocean
My best friend is a lake
Because we are gentle, we like to play tag
My enemy is the sun
Because it can evaporate me
I fear pollution
Because it can hurt me
I love the fish
Because they swim in me
I dream (or wish) to be like my dad and mom, like an ocean and a river

Baseball
by Donald Dobeck III

Baseball is a sport I like to play in the spring
You can almost hear the sting of the bat, ding!
There's a ball heading right for the fence
I hope there is a good defense!
The pitcher throws a circle change
That pitch is mysterious and strange
There was a swing and a miss!
It's almost like the pitcher made a diss!
You could feel the breeze
As the pitcher threw the ball with ease!
The ball is going right to second base
Quick, you only have a few seconds to throw it to first base

Springtime
by Julia Boutchie

Super
Pretty flowers grow
Rain and storms start to come
Imagine what fun you have
Nice to be outside
Girls' softball starts
Time to ride bikes
Incredible fun you have
My favorite season
Excited-ness starts

What Is Green?
by Charlotte Cabot

Green is iguanas or Easter grass
Green is a turtle, go fast
Green is a lime that makes your drink tart
Green is an apple that is unripe
Green is a clover soft in the grass
Green is a sign I often pass
Green is a leaf before it turns brown
Green is the color of my home town

Social Studies (Explorers)
by Jessica Carter

Learn about explorers
Who sailed the seven seas
Or tell about Christopher Columbus
Who went to the Indies
Or write about Cortez
Who conquered the Aztecs just for gold
Well, that's what I've been told
Explorers are important
For you and me
They are a part of our human history!

Water and Rainbow
by Chuckie Kirk

I am a water drop, you know me for the rainbow I create
My mother is a drop of water from the rainforest
My father is a drop of water from the woods
I was born on a farm, I live in water
My best friend is a water drop, because he is nice, and we like to swim
My enemies are electricity and lightning because they shock me
I fear humans because they toxify me
I love making rainbows because they are beautiful
I dream of world peace

I Am
by Austin Brown

I am a computer
You know me for my web searches
My father is the memory
I was born in a factory
I live in homes of people and classes in schools
My best friend is electricity because I run by it
We like to run together
My enemies are viruses because they mess up my programming
I fear power surges because they turn me off
I love new programs because they are awesome
I dream to be used by the President

The Stray
by Daymen Hodge

With sooty black fur, an excited stray pup sat on my porch
Looking through the screen door
The hound cried out to me until I let him come inside
I was so happy!
Mom was okay until my pooch chewed up her shoes
Chewing up my mom's shoes! Oh, please stop!
"I will not be able to keep him," I thought
"How can I keep you when you have made Mom really mad?"
To my surprise, my mom let me keep him, she just took him outside
My dog, Harley, is 4 years old now
A Labrador retriever, his fur is still sooty black
Harley was a very small puppy when he was about two months old
But now he is very large
He was a stray, then a guest and finally, my own dog
To my surprise, Harley is like a brother
When I come home, Harley jumps and licks my face
Harley is a playful dog, always wanting to go for a walk
Always begging for a treat, and always playing with toys
Harley never chews on Mom's shoes anymore
Once a guest, but now my own dog

Reunited
by Cameron Skinner

You are gone
I wish I could have been there
To hold your hand and tell you it will be okay
But I wasn't
Before I knew it, you were gone
Darkness enveloped me like a cloud
All the happy memories we shared
Shattered like broken glass
But in the midst of all the emotions, I remembered
Someday, together for always, reunited we shall be
- In memory of my grandma, Marilyn Merris, who passed away in July of 2003

Where I'm From
by Shelby Jones

I am from a scary house
From scary neighbors and creaky floors
I am from an old oak tree
Which sits behind the scary neighbor's house
I am from leaky roofs and a basement pitch black
I'm from a house where people are out of control
I'm from the floor beneath you
And when you wake up you don't want to walk on the floor
I'm from two people and they torture me a whole lot
They make me eat beets and lima beans
You know who those two people are
There, coming from beneath my bed is a terrifying sound
You know what happens next

Family
by Greta O'Marah

Friendly as a kitten
Always there for me
Marvelous as an eagle
Interesting as a peacock
Loves like a robin
You couldn't live without one

Speeder Bike
by Kody Rainwater

I am a Speeder bike
You know me for speed
My mother is metal
My father is a handle
I was born in a factory
I live indoors
My best friend is shield bunker because he is made of metal
We like to talk
My enemies are trees because I can die
I fear getting shot because I can die
I love heart medication because it tastes good
I dream to make friends

I Am a Carefree Horse Lover
by Jeffrey Staton

I am a carefree horse lover
I wonder if my horse will always be a champion racehorse
I hear the wind blow past me
I ride the champion racehorse
I see the champion racehorse in a gold saddle
I want to ride the champion through the valley
I am a carefree horse lover
I pretend to be a champion horse rider
I feel the wind blowing my hair
I touch the wind because we are going so fast
I worry that we will ride over a rocky cliff while ride through the green grass
I cry when a horse becomes all
I am a carefree horse lover
I understand that my racehorse will not always be a racehorse
I say let all the horses have a good home
I dream my champion racehorse is having a baby champion racehorse
I try to be a loving horse lover all my life
I hope to race the champion racehorse all my life
I am a carefree horse lover

The Flame
by Zach Johnson

I am the flame
You know me for my light and my warmth
My mother is heat, my father is spark
I was born in the darkness, I made light
I live for spreading and burning
My best friend is the wind
Because he makes me spread
My enemy is water, my cool flowing foe
Because she puts out my flame
And darkens my light
I fear the rain, the snow and sleet
Because they cool my heat, which causes defeat
I love the forest because I can spread and spread
I dream to never burn out and to flame forever

I Am a Boy Who Loves My Family
by Wally Fraley

I'm a nice boy who loves my family
I wonder when I grow up if I can travel to another state
I hear something climbing in the trees
I see a stop sign as I travel
I want my own house when I grow up
I am a nice boy who loves my family
I pretend I am a doctor who can help
I feel good when I help everyone
I touch the moon when in my bed at night
I worry when I have bad dreams
I cry when I adopt a bro in Cincinnati
I am a nice boy who loves my family
I understand that after I graduate, I will get a job
I say everyone should be good to everyone
I dream of growing up to be a baseball player
I try to hit a home run when I play baseball
I hope that I am on a team when I grow up
I am a nice boy who loves my family

Ryan's Sign
by Jacob A. Cecil

Ryan Pine had a great time
I see a sign
Mine!
That's fine

I Am a Snake
by Shea Sherman

I am a python snake
You know me for my smooth slither
My mother is a snake, my father is also
I was born in the woods, I live in a tree
My best friend is a snake, because we're friends
We like to climb trees, my enemy is a copperhead
Because we do stuff together
I fear a copperhead, because they are mean
I love my family, because they are fun and I love them
I dream that I was a real snake

I Am a Rose
by Bethany Meeks

I am a rose, you know me for my beauty
My mother is a tulip, just like her mother
My father is a dandelion, just like his father
I was born in a garden, I live in a park
My best friend is a sunflower, because she grows next to me
We like to blow in the wind
My enemy is the hard wind, because it can blow me away
I fear the snow because it is ice-cold
I love the sun because it helps me grow
I dream to have an even sweeter scent

Me, Myself, and I
by Kimberly Schoener

From my head to my toes, I am beautiful
Not caring what everyone thinks of me
Not being told what to do or say
Just being the way I am
Beautiful comes from within, from your soul
From what you think of yourself
Beautiful is whether or not you love yourself
So if you don't love yourself
You, and all the people around you, won't think you're beautiful

The Baby Moose Is On the Loose
by Raychel Kazee

Oh, the baby moose is on the loose
But the baby moose is always loose
The baby moose had a loose tooth
He is loose, too
Nobody can be loose with a wild moose
Nobody can live with a loose moose with a loose tooth
Well, the moose lost his tooth and went totally loose
When he lost his tooth, he still was a little loose on the moose
Well, he knocked another tooth loose
Then he went berserk
He went so berserk he hit a tree
Then he tripped over a rock

I Am
by Ashley Delong

I am a butterfly
You know me for protection
My mother is beautiful
My father is brave
I was born in a forest
I live in a tree
My best friend is a caterpillar
Because we like to play, we like to make jokes
My enemy is a bird, because birds like to eat butterflies
I fear birds, because they can be sneaky
I love my mother, because she knows what to do
I wish I could be just like her

Summer
by Kaitlyn Burks

It is summer
I see beautiful colored flowers growing at the side of my house
Families at the beach swimming in the salty warm water
And bright green leaves on the tall oak tree in my front yard
It is summer
I smell beautiful sweet pink tulips I pick for my mom
Spicy barbeque chicken legs cooking on the grill
And fresh mowed green grass that my dad just cut
It is summer
I taste yummy blueberries that my mom puts in a bowl for me
Sweet apple juice that runs down my face when I eat an apple
And yummy green fresh grapes from the grocery store
It is summer
I feel round bouncing basketballs as I play with my friends
Cold clear water that I jumped in to get cooled off after getting hot and sweaty
And the wind from a smooth ride on my light blue bike
Down a big hill near my house
It is summer
I hear splashing sounds from the children playing in their pool
The chirping of happy blue birds outside in my backyard
And people playing and laughing outside in their front yard

I Am
by Madison Derr

I am a thesaurus
You know me for my meanings
My mother is the dictionary
My father is the library
I was born in someone's mind
I live through the paper
My best friend is a book
Because it has words
We like to share our feelings
My enemy is an incinerator
Because it burns books
I fear fire
Because it can destroy me
I love fingers
Because they help me feel things
I wish I was a human

I Am
by Madison Goble

I am a nice boy
I love to ride
I love to write
I love to fish
I am a nice boy
I love to play
I love to hunt
I love to do homework
I love school
I am a nice boy
I have my friends
I have to go places
I have to go out
I am a nice boy
I have to go to the beach
I have cats
I have dogs
I am a nice boy
I love my family
I love to walk
I love to watch TV
I am a nice boy

Runner Up

Alexandra Mardirossian

A member of both her school and all county choirs,
Alexandra also enjoys tennis and playing the flute.
Big sister to a pair of five year olds,
she still finds time to pursue lessons in a second language.
We appreciate Alexandra's heartwarming tribute to her Grandpa,
and know that he must have been very proud
of his talented Granddaughter.

My Grandpa
by Alexandra Mardirossian

My grandpa was a quiet man
He was not wild or weak
He was like a willow in the breeze, swaying gracefully
While we are loud, he was soft
He was as peaceful as a light snow drifting down on a leaf
He was a caterpillar who went into his cocoon
He left his shell, his body, on Earth
Now he is a butterfly
His soul wanders freely

Michelle Krumpe

This delightful young lady was in the 5th grade
when she decided to write a few magical lines
about the favorite flowers that grace her garden.
Michelle forgot to mention in her poem
that she has the pleasure
of trying to chase a total of six pet rabbits
and a chinchilla out of that garden on a regular basis.
If the bunnies are behaving themselves,
Michelle is either off to the mall
or biking to the store for ice cream.

Snapdragons
by Michelle Krumpe

Nestled 'neath a bush so snug and warm
Waiting for the light of day
The little snapdragons sit forlorn
While the fairies with the roses play
She wishes she could fly like them
So free and full of light
She watches as their glow comes near
But then it's gone, and out of sight

Division II

Grades 6-7

The Comeback Limerick
by Wesley Trask

The Red Sox were down three and oh
Their chances of winning were low
They hit a homerun
The fans had some fun
But they still had three games to go

Penguin
by Alexander Gates

He waddles like a duck in snow
He sleds as fast as he can go
And swims as if in a water show
Orange beak, webbed feet, and has fins
He may not fly but can do spins
A sport at fishing always wins

Why?
by Jesica Garcia

Why do teenagers think it's cool to fly high?
Why do they only realize the truth as they're about to die?
Why do most people like to smoke?
Why does it cause people to cough and others to choke?
Why did the Twin Towers have to crash?
Why did innocent bodies have to turn into ash?
Why does racism still exist?
Why does life have to be something we cannot resist?
Why can't people accept others for what they wear?
Why do people stare at others as if they were rare?
Why do people do mean things to others and not care?
Why is almost everything in life so unfair?
Why do people not notice they pollute?
Why do people always like to take the easy route?
Why did Hurricane Katrina have to attack us?
Why did so many people have to leave us?
Why are most preteens in a rush to grow?
Why are most preteens' self-esteems so low?
Why do the people we love have to go?
These are 19 questions we'll never know

Last Words
by Alex Serrazina

There I was on that fateful day, my heart was racing
Wasn't sure how I was going to handle it
Walking through the revolving door, whoosh, whoosh
I prepare for the worst; a single tear drop fell on his forehead
My dad died, I remember his last words, "Alex, I love you"

Never Play To the Extremities
by Kenneth Scott

Sometime ago in a kingdom by the sea
Lived a man name Benny Bell B
Benny Bell B knows a Mcar Sherie
And Mcar Sherie lives by a tree
Mcar Sherie is wearing a white tee
If you look closely you can see it says dictionary
Benny Bell B and Mcar Sherie were playing by the sea
When Benny Bell B fell and hurt his knee
Benny Bell B went to a hospital by the sea
Name Hospital of Emergency
When the doctor asked Benny what happened, he said, "I was playing by the sea
And fell and broke my knee"
Then the doctor said, "Yes, I can see"
So then the doctor helped him heal his knee
The doctor said, "No more playing to the extremities"
Benny went back to school after three weeks, and he won the spelling bee
Benny Bell B told his mommy and she said, "That's lovely"
He gave her a daisy
For his accomplishment, Benny's friend Mcar Sherie
Through a get-together, which is called a house party
Benny's brother Stinkami Hairy
Had a party six weeks later because he turned three
Benny ended up having to pay his doctor's fee
He finally finished college where he studied archeology
A month and a week after that, Benny's mom said, "Here's your key
For your new car since you just turned twenty-three"
Along the way he met a woman named Mariey (Ma-ri-ee)
Whom he married, now he calls her "Wifey"
He had three children name Jeff, Mary, and Sniffey (Sni-fee)
Benny lived happily ever after to the age of 23
How would you live your life if you lived here?
Would you expect it to turn out this way?

Virginia
by Robert Salter

In Virginia it's fun to have fun
With family and friends
My family has a bunny
It likes to runny
It's very funny
There's plenty of space to run
Plenty of animals to pet
There are a few cousins I haven't met yet
They have a pool
It's really cool
You can ride your ATV
Or chill and watch MTV
You feel very free
Just be whoever you want to be
They have cows; I taught it how to bow
The cow still won't meow
In Kung Fu hustle it goes, "Pow!"
And I'm all like, "Wow!"

Thoroughbreds
by Lori Smith

You are fast and free
You run furiously with joyful glee
You charge through a challenging course
And you make the right choice
Sometimes you are running furiously down the track
With the anxious rider you pack
You must do your very best
To pass the difficult test
Thoroughbreds are the fastest of their kind
When you are racing, you are in a tight bind
When your hooves hit the ground, it shakes
If you love to run, that is all it takes
If you keep up the fast pace
You will win the long awaited race
When you have won, and you are coming down the track
I'll lay a beautiful blanket of roses on your back
One day I will own a Thoroughbred like you
And I will turn you out into a Kentucky field of blue
You will have a nice warm stable when it is cold
You will live here till you grow old

Time
by Steven Towne

It can weather away a mountain
It can cause a rising sea
It can make a man grow older, and make new technology
What force can fill the ground with snow?
Or make grass as green as a lime?
The only force I am talking about is the mystical power of time

Excuses
by Erica Lang

When I didn't do my homework, my teacher asked why
I felt like a jerk and as small as a fly
I had good excuses ready in my head
Like the one when my homework crawled under my bed
I wished I could leave in the blink of an eye
Or maybe be disguised as Boston cream pie
I felt so misunderstood
Because one excuse was good
But I probably won't remember till the 4th of July
Even if I did, I wouldn't give it a try
I was ready to reply that my homework could fly
But then I thought maybe homework could die
Next time I'll give it a better try

I Dream of My Old Life
by Courtney Curry

My heart beating fast as the blood runs through my veins
What's going on, nothing seems the same
Is this a dream or is it something real?
Can I really touch, or can I only feel?
Life seems so awkward as if it's always ending
Does no one ever really get the vibe that everyone's sending?
My eyes racing ponderously, around in circles they go
Where is this life taking me, that I will never know
As the alarm sounds, I solemnly open my eyes
Slowly I look around, as I tell my old life goodbye

Horses
by Kimmy Strickland

Trotting in the ring
Canter in the field
Walking through the hall
Seeing the horses
Quarter horse, paint
Bay, stallion, foal
Bridle makes Ray look like a saint
Yankee, black as coal

Games
by Olivia Wise

Monopoly, Mouse Trap, Life
Clue, Sorry, Trouble
Rolling dice, going from start to finish
Moving my piece across the board
Counting my money, hoping I prevail
But this game will soon come to an end
When everybody loses, and I win!

Cousins We Are, Sisters We Wish
by Cena Cherry

I would be lonesome without my cousin, my friend
I go and see her every weekend, together, since the day we were born
Cousins we are, sisters we wish
We always sing and dance, and dream of love and romance
We grew a special bond at the ages of seven and nine
Our friendship will never decline
Cousins we are, sisters we wish
We used to have sleepovers all the time; we never did commit a crime
We act alike, look alike, and think the same
These similarities never brought us any shame
Cousins we are, sisters we wish
Our family realizes our closeness; our relationship will never be worthless
Our family is growing, just like us, now we always make a promise
Cousins we are, sisters we wish

The Backyard
by Charlotte Gruenberg

A forest of trees, yet only ten stand
Millions of squirrels, yet only five scurry
Billions of birds, yet only fifteen fly
Hundreds of flowers, yet only thirty bloom
We all see creations of nature
As more than they really are
It's the beauty that makes it seem like more

The Portal To the Past
by Daniel Lazour

History is the past, whether it's a minute, an hour, or a year ago
History grows as time passes by; history will never die
A bank filled with events and people from the dawn of time
To the Wall Street crash, history stores all the cash
Washington, Caesar, Aristotle, all have their place
An amazing portal through time, history will take you there

Goal!
by Nathan Stark

I shot a puck in the net
While falling and getting wet
In, in it went, hitting post to post
As the goalie was so, so, so close
Goal, goal, goal, it was looking bright
It was an amazing, special sight

Why?
by Chris Phillips

He's at his house crying
Why is he crying?
Because our people go to war, now they're dying
Make it the last time
Why, tell me why, people go to war?
All it is, is a death door

Dreams
by Taciane Santos

People have lots of dreams
They go on forever like streams
They fight for what they believe
So they can always achieve
In dreams, people feel like big stars
If they keep on believing, it will be the size of Mars
Dreams are shiny and bright like clouds
But in the end, you will always be proud
Some people want to be models and teachers
But others want to be actors and speakers
Dreaming is all about believing
So if you believe, you will succeed

Mornings
by Gretchen Gessner

Waking up is like getting up from a two minute snooze, hard and undesirable
You want to just slap those cotton covers over your head and ignore everyone else
Dark, damp, eerie morning
But licks from your dogs, wanting you to wake up fast, give you a sweet smile
Maybe you wake up to yummy smells of your mom's home cooking
Which makes waking up from your snooze worth it

The Falling Mist
by Miranda Peege

It flows down, down the stream
I follow it, jumping from rock to rock
Trying not to fall into the crystal blue water
No rocks to aid
I step into the water, it reaches my knees
I notice that it is way too deep
I continue backward my steps to safe land
I keep on following the soft moving water
It comes to an end, reaching the waterfall
I look down the river
It flows in sheets of silk to the pool of crystal blue water

Penguins
by Kate Yoder

Waddle, waddle, dive, eat
Look out world
Oh wait, it's just me
This world is fantastic
Filled with blue water, crystal clear ice
All just for me, all the sights I can see
Enormous yellow rays cast down on me
The food tastes great; all the fish I get to eat
And look, there's my little brother's egg, getting ready to break

Wanderer
by Thompson Zhang

I am a wanderer, a wanderer of the night
I am looking for my dream, the one that means a lot to me
I walk the dusty roads, I follow the moonlit night
I walk with stars and have companions
I talk with no one and no one talks to me
I walk with no one long enough to call us, "we"
My path is long and twisted
I will not have any time wasted, until I find my goal
I am a wanderer, a wanderer of the night
I need to find my dream at the first light
The starry skies point the way I walk until my dream is found
But I have not found it, I am still walking

Sometimes
by Maya Saunders

Sometimes I cry and I don't know why
Sometimes I sing about silly things
Sometimes I wish you were dead and you were brain dead
But sometimes I love you and I want to cry
Sometimes you're funny and a big dummy
Sometimes you make me mad and very sad
Sometimes you hurt me without even knowing it
Sometimes I cry and wish you were mine
Sometimes you're my everything

Death
by Leah Gellineau

A tear, a single, salty tear
The end near, but there is more to come
For when he's done, when he's through
No, I can't forgive you, I loved him
His face held all the colors of the rainbow
His smile held the joy of thousands
In him was all the love in the world
Now lost forever, in the unforgiving clutches of death

America
by Cody Abbott

America, land of the free
Where all walks of people can be
A country so the same, yet full of diversity
Where people are accepted
And connected
Where a child's new life can begin
With parents of a different skin
America you have been good to me
Not every year or month, but day
America you certainly have your faults
But I would not have you any other way

Life Is ...
by Amber Szpyrka

Life is like day and night, once it is there, then it is gone
Big and bright, small and dull
Life is like a dream, full of ideas and thoughts
Then it disappears for good; you're gone, lifeless
Life is like a sunflower
Big, beautiful, colorful, and bright
You know you are just right
Life is like a roller coaster, you have hills
And go off into high places, then it just vanishes
Life ... you never know when or where it will take you, it just will

My Brother, Kevin
by Emily Heaney

Kevin, misunderstood by others
No words, only sound
Calm, but hyper, too
Innocent smile, the best laugh
Has a different way of learning
Sign language and pictures are his only way of communicating
Brain disorder, autism

Get Up and Dance
by Brittney Bellamy

Dancing is like art for the soul, makes you feel good
When you're down, if you're the only person in the room, you can do the disco duck
Or, if you are feeling really rowdy, you can find a partner and just slow dance
Get up and dance!
Dancing can relax your mind after a hard and nerve-racking day
Dancing can make you feel like you're floating on air
Or dancing is like flying through the air, or having the wind blow through your hair
Get up and dance!
I know this may sound crazy, but dancing is fun for everyone
When I was little, I used to think I was too young to learn how to do anything
But then I gave it a try, and now I don't want to stop!
Dancing can be spiritual, or you can just have fun with it!
So get up and dance!

That Ain't Cool
by Micaela Donoghue

Everyone thinks they're so cool
They've got their pants down to their knees
Jeez, everybody freeze, that ain't cool
He walks through the door, his pants ten sizes too big
He thinks he looks cool, but he looks like a pig, that ain't cool
Look at her shirt, it's up to her bellybutton, you think people wanna see that?
You think it looks cool, but it makes you look fat, that ain't cool
Your pants, they're so tight, you need to grow up and get a life
You're not five no more, you're out of that size
You need to start being yourself, and stop tryin' to impress the guys
That ain't cool!

How Happy Is Happy?
by Katherine Cronin

Happiness comes in all shapes and sizes
Happiness is like apple pie
So yummy and warm in my mouth
It's also like seeing people and saying, "Hi"
Christmas is like happiness
Seeing my family saying, "Oh me, oh my!"
But the real question is, how happy is happy?

Blizzard
by Farrah Beaubrun

A whirlwind of snow makes driving impossible
Making this disaster a hazard to vision
We try to see, but all we can do it turn on the double signal lights
Cold, shivering in the car
Like the snow slowly seeps into the window
To make us shiver in pain

Blue and White
by Ernie Gurish

Why is it blue? Must it be true?
I don't understand, why be so bland?
Why are they white? It's not like they bite
Around they float, just like a boat
In that heavenly ocean of blue
So in that blue, the white splotch floats through
Running from that big endless ol' blue
So then why be blue? I haven't a clue
Why be white as they sail like kites
Within that big ol' blue

Something Nobody Wants To Do
by Bobby White

He was sad
He could no longer play
He knew he had to move on
He had to live on his own
He had grown up

Star
by Shauna Vespa

As I watch soldiers going off to war
I think of how brave they really are
Watching a fire fighter climbing up a ladder
Makes me even sadder
I see police fighting terrible crimes
This makes me want to cry sometimes
But as I sit and stare
But only try to glare
I know they're fighting for our stars

Killer Whale
by Kylan Nelson

Move swiftly through the liquid, into the depths of loneliness
Water crawling all around him, as he slips by through the water
His neighbors scamper away, the small seal calls out in pain
These creatures see him as a killer, so he slowly swims away
Oh, but wait, as he glides, slides, rides, he encounters a new feeling
Not rage, raw, or riot, he feels curious, like a little puppy
Because many others see him as a gentle giant
Still gliding, he hears a new sound, a screech
That batters the silence, a wave of hope, rippling through the darkness
He feels, knows, he is not alone

Dancing Shoes
by Alexandra Hepfinger

Tall and lanky at first glance
I stare into the mirror and tell myself, "Just one chance"
My costume is on, my hair transformed into a tight bun
It's my turn next, and there is nowhere to run
I'm on stage; the lights are hot and bright
When the curtain opens, I fancy with delight
Five, six, seven, eight, I listen to the beat
And pray so do my feet
My dance shoes take over, I'm in my element now
I have no fear; I'm doing what I love now
Sashay into a leap, jazz-walking across the stage
Turning one, two, three, the crowd's eyes are all on me

My Papaw, My Friend
by Summer Browning

There he is, my papaw
Snow white hair, topped off with a cap
Upon his gentle face golden spectacles rest serenely
His faded, tattered coveralls match his worn, western boots
Trademarks of his appearance as he walks across his land
There he is, my papaw, my papaw is a worker
Diligent to life's demands, he's friendly and reliable
Quick to offer a helping hand to neighbors far and near
Everyone who knows him says, "There goes a wonderful man"
There he is, my papaw, whom I also call my friend
Always there for me through the thick and through the thin
His loving ways are obvious for everyone to see
Sometimes it's in his smile or his laughter soft and low
Other times it's in his eyes, hazel orbs that seem to glow
There he is, my papaw, with an affection for me that no one can take away
He spoils me rotten that's for sure, as he plays with me all day
It is no wonder; in fact, it's plain to see why I set him above the rest
My papaw is my friend and he truly is the best!

Only a Thought
by Ryan Gioffre

If someone gets hit, should I stand up and fight?
Be seen in the light, use all my might?
Don't run away, even if I can?
Or run away and never come back again?
Just thinking, only a thought
What could I have done? Maybe a lot
But who knows? It's only a thought
What if it was a lie?
Should I own up to it and say I am sorry?
Do what I can to make it right again?
Or should I back down and sleep with a quilt of guilt?
Just thinking, only a thought
What could I have done? Maybe a lot
But who knows? It's only a thought
What if it was a thought?
What if I thought I saw something I really did not see?
That just reminds me
Believe nothing of what you hear and half of what you see
But just thinking, don't mind me
It's only a thought, not something you should believe
Only a thought

Anywhere, Just You and Me
by Sarah McFadden

Oh won't you come out and play with me?
It's a beautiful day you see
We can go to the sea
Just you and me
We could go to the beach
We could even teach!
You and I could go to see the killer whale Shamoo
Or even go to Timbuktu!
We could go anywhere
The beach, the mountains
Anywhere you know
Just you and me
Oh, we could just go
Anywhere you see
Just you and me!

Shore of Memories
by Varsha Muralidhar

I watch as my memories wash upon my battered shores
They gleam in the sunlight as they evaporate
I shed tears trying to remember what should be forgotten
I grab the thin air as though trying to catch what I have forgotten
And place it in my soul
I know I cannot cling to these memories, I know they must be set free
For, one day they shall return to tear apart my gentle heart
To confuse my tender soul and help make more
More memories

Mustang Spirit
by Alexa Santamaria

I hear the sound of the wind
And the bump, bump, bump of its hooves
It gallops as fast as it could possibly race
And soon it will fly, soar like an eagle
It looks so happy and free as it rises to the sky
It's not just the symbol of Kentucky
It's the meaning and definition of the greatest place to be
So, when you hear that sound, it will fill you with love and happiness!

They Have Nothing I Want
by Bailey Rose

Eyes like a snake's
They watch you shake
Fierce fire in their hearts
Drip, drip, dew falls from my forehead
As I crumble, they get stronger
Weakened by the stress
Can't run, can't hide
In a powwow as if Indians
They mutter collectively with a wall up
They think you can't see
Together, wicked and vicious
Apart, powerless and fragile
They despise each other, not just you
And I see they have nothing I want

A Tear
by Connor Jackson

A time of sorrow
So, how did we deserve this?
What I see now is
A frown upon a great beak
A tear on the eagle's cheek

Leaving It Behind
by Rachel Hill

Down from my eye came a tear, a trickle of running water
My heart cracked as my belongings were stowed in cardboard boxes
In Louisville, Kentucky they were destined to be unpacked
I worried, not knowing what it would be like, would I fit in?
The Chinese men picking up boxes; how small, lean, but strong they were
The eerie feeling of an empty room echoing for the very first time
I had not cast this sight for many a year
The last of the boxes were departing; three, two, one, they're gone
The truck was already rumbling away, there was no coming back
My hands were quivering as I reach for my mom like I was still a small child
Once again the running tap, drip, drip, drip from my eye

Animals
by Alexandria Blunt

A walrus and a hippopotamus are fat
Not like a cat or a bat
They need fitness help
A dog will yelp
Now if you don't see a cow
Don't meow or growl, for it will be on the prowl
If you see a pig
It will be very big
They eat a lot of food though they think they should
A butterfly can say bye-bye
And is very sly
If you see a fox inside a box
It's probably hiding clocks
If you see a seal in high heels
It likes hot meals

My Valentine Spirit
by Emily Isaacs

You're in my every valentine, my every single wish
I can never really see you, but I know you're there, so I know you care
I always hate the darkness, but when you're around
The darkness is filled with light, and silence is filled with sound
I always will love you, though you've passed away
I will see you again, on my last day

Poem
by Mary Fulham

Let it eat you
Let it curl you up into a tiny ball and totally creep you out
Let the words roll off your tongue into a field of harmony and sun
Let it take you over, it is more powerful than you are
So give in before it kills you in your own special way
Let it sing to you, believe me
The song of words that it sings is too great for you to resist
Let it look inside you and tell you what you need to know
It will figure out your secrets, it is wiser than you
Let it speak to you, if you read between the lines
It is so beautiful that you will then truly understand its true meaning

Unwanted Party
by Kelsey Page

The faint but lovely smell fills my nose
Waiting anxiously to see the cake
I open my eyes
Ahh!
"It is so cool," I said
Suddenly a horrible feeling clouds over me
It darkens the room
My stomach knots up
Not knowing what to do
I get dizzy
I realized
This was the party I never wanted to have
It was my going away party

I'm Thankful For ...
by Ilena Burnett

I'm thankful for
All my friends and family who are always by my side
And with me through happy and sad times
I'm thankful for police men all around me who fight off crime
I'm thankful for the house I live in and the school I go to
I'm thankful for everything, but most of all I'm thankful for you!

My Symphony
by Cameron Naglieri-Prescod

The night crawls into the sky, the lights dim and a small light lit the room
I sit down on the dark red oak bench, and open the covering
I hit a note on the ivory keys, then another one
I hit several chords in my symphony, and the notes and chords join together
As the light was brightening, I play louder and faster, and I see demons on the walls
The blood coming from their mouths, as I can hear them scream in terror
The door is disappearing, and the scarlet and brick red blood is rising with the song
This scene is horrifying, and the blood is up to my chest
My ears, oh I wish I could cut them off!
The blood is almost to my neck now; the blood is coming out of the keys
I am right at the end of my symphony, and then ... nothing
The music and blood stop; finally, I am finished with my symphony

My Adventure
by Amanda Garceau

I wanted to do something, anything at all
Instead of just staying here and learning about Neanderthal
I wanted to have an adventure, hike, run, and swim
But I can't, because I have to learn a synonym
It's boring in school, all you do is sit
It was then I decided, I would quit
I ran out of school before the bell rung
And that is when my adventure begun
I ran down the road into a dark alley
When I realized I was missing the pep rally
I ran to get there but then got a cramp
And fell to the ground, where it was all damp
I woke up with a big headache
I felt my brain just had an earthquake
I ran back to school and realized I do care
But when I got there, it was over, no fair!

Colors
by Taylor Cline

Like a box of crayons, our world is filled with many vivid colors
Hues of every shade and tint appear without warning, without alarm
But the beauty of all these colors tell a story of change
Night to day, summer to fall, life to death
Our world is a colorful drawing that has come to life
Colors, all kinds of colors- some light, some dark, some bright, some dull
Colors, all colors, emerge in nature
The night sky dark and black filled with twinkling white stars
A blanket of pure white snow meets the horizon of a dreary gray sky
The brilliant golden sun shines on a crystal blue ocean creating a sea of diamonds
A rose of deep ruby red blooms slowly on a bush surrounded by thorns
And bright emerald leaves, the cool crisp breeze dances through the trees
As leaves of intense red and pumpkin orange float
To the green and brown earth below
Like a rainbow stretched across the sky
Our planet is created by many stunning colors
A spectrum of every shade and tint appear without notice, without caution
But the beauty of these colors tell a story of change
Night to day, summer to fall, life to death
Our world is a colorful rainbow that has come to life

Adventure
by Ashley Hart

Climbing up a tree is like an adventure
Fun, high, windy, and cool
Taking one step at a time
Higher, higher, here I go!
Oops! Hit my head
Climbing a tree is like an adventure
Climbing a tree is like an adventure
Leaves, air, so much nature everywhere
Hear the birds singing melodies
Singing, singing everywhere
Few more steps, nearly there
Climbing a tree is like an adventure
Climbing a tree is like an adventure
Leaves, leaves, so many leaves
Left, right, everywhere
More, more, more fall down
I'm there, it's so high
Climbing a tree is an adventure

Just Be Yourself
by Kelsey Coates

I am from a place of love
Where hearts of others touch your own
Where a small word could change everyone and everything around you
I come from a place of caring
Where moms and dads ask how your day was
From a place where everyone is a part of everybody's life
Where nobody is left out of the never-ending circle
I come from a place of trust
Where you can ask upon another person to keep a secret
Where you can feel secure without protecting yourself
I come from a place of strength
Where I don't have to change who I am to be strong
I am from a family, a family that loves, cares, trusts, hopes, and dreams
A family that gives independence and strength
But most of all, a family that lets me be myself
I can believe what I want, I can laugh how and when I want
I can follow my own path, I can be myself; not somebody else

Fishing
by Cameron Dutt

A day almost anyone can enjoy
(Cast)
A day on the lake with your father
(Splash)
A day for relaxing and enjoying life
(Reel)
A day you hope never ends
(Bite)
A day you cherish family
(Reel harder)
A day that feels like a dream
(Almost there)
A day you will remember forever
(Got it)
And a day you catch your first fish

Basketball
by Maddie Naylor

An orange globe spinning, like a shining sun
Longitude and latitude lines, a map showing the way
Flying through the air, jumping to and fro
A tiny collection of mountains, a confusing mini maze
A Halloween pumpkin, glowing with a blaze
A hard bumpy orange, with a sly mysterious smile
Dancing around the court, going through a netted hoop
And falling hard on the ground with a thump

Cars
by Craig Gordnier

Rims as big as the sun
Spinning as fast as the speed of light
Fiery fast Ferrari
Perfect performance Porsche
Running like the wind
Blurring one's vision like the hardest eye test
A soaring golden eagle
Cars are the ingredients to an adrenalin rush
Hugging the road like a little girl with a new teddy bear

An Idea
by Evan Supple

Unstoppable, unbreakable, unreliable
An idea is perfect in the mind
An idea is flawless in design
An idea is everything yet nothing
An idea is what drives life
An idea is what causes war
An idea is what causes love
An idea is the world
An idea is the universe
An idea is a theory
A brainstorm, a mind charge, a ruler

My Fish
by Drew Ison

My line went into a pine tree
My fishhook hooked my book, but not my fish
The bass which was itchy, flippy, smelly
And had a big belly, full of grape jelly
Inside its belly, pink and smelly

Siren
by Kene Onyekwuluje

The cops are coming
I'm running
They see me on my street
I've used up my feet, like last week's QB sneak
The cops are comin'
The neighbors are humming
They see me in a car
It's been two hours so far, I have two scars
The cops are coming; they see me on a train
I've still got the same pain; I'm on the B-train
I've got two shirt stains
They see me on the plane, I feel the same
I was caught on the hook
I've closed my book

What If?
by Bradley Snay

What if the world were square?
What if people didn't care?
What if TV wasn't invented?
What if cars weren't vented?
What if we didn't exist?
What if we couldn't resist?
Things could get crazy, just don't be lazy

Cat
by Alec Horn

Calming, charming, cuddly
Strides outside, glares around
Spots a bird, lunchtime, creeps around
Low to the ground, like an army man
Tracks the bird, pounces, attacks
Wrestles, kills, lunch is served
Calm, charming, cuddly
Sometimes vicious

Candy
by Philina Lor

Sweet ol' candy
You never fail me, oh dandy
Yummy gumdrops
And delicious sugar pops
Cookies are cool
But candy's the one that makes you drool
Ice cream, licorice, vanilla, too
Cinnamon can give you a clue
That chocolate is quite sure
It can heal your trouble
Or just make your sickness double
Scrumptious sweets
And tasty treats
Will make you crave it
Just as much as an ocean's salty wave

Who To Be
by Kaitlyn Jacobsen

Who am I to be?
A doctor, a preacher, or even a banker?
Am I the marrying type or will I be single for the rest of my life?
Will I have 12 kids or none?
Am I going to be in movies or living on the street?
I don't know
I'm only 13 and looking for someone with answers
Can you tell me am I going to have fame or be the one to blame?
Maybe you can; maybe you can't
Just thought I'd ask if you had some answers on who I am to be

Saturday Morning, and a Cloud In the Sky
by Jake Saltzman

The covers double over, and another day awakes
Downstairs there is bacon, sausage, and pancakes
In the den jazz plays with that same consistent Saturday morning beat
Even if you don't want to, you can't help but tap your feet
Hockey game in the morning, college football's on at night
Everybody looking for that Kansas and Pittsburgh upset, yeah right!
The fork hits the plate and bounces off metal with a ping
Then I'm headed outside with money in my pocket making its "ching-ching"
I head for the store where I need a paper
And mayoral candidate's eye-appealing green pin
That is when I glance up at the sky, sun beaming off my chin
Only one cloud floating solo up in the air
But I realize there is something special about this one, and finally it's all clear
That one cloud represents more than a liquid, solid, and gas
That cloud represents all of us
And everyone who celebrates Saturday mornings with class

Raised Hairs
by Stephen Parker

What raises your hairs, what raises mine?
What makes us scared, that death thinks is divine?
Is it the sounds of ghosts in the halls?
Is it the sound we make when the reaper calls?
Is it the sounds they make in their heads?
What raises your hairs, what raises mine?
What's going on in our little minds?

Hat
by Zachary Hall

Hats cover your head
I suggest you don't wear one in bed
They're comfy and good-looking
You might find them hooking
They come in red, green, brown, and blue
Trust me, this is all true
Animal hats, people hats, plant hats, too
You just have to find the right hat for you

Why?
by Caroline Griffin

Why do we think these people are our friends?
They talk about us, it never ends
Those people, yeah, right over there
Why do they laugh? Why do they stare?
Stand up for what you believe
It's not your thoughts who deceive
Even if they don't understand
Still keep control, you're in demand
It's your opinion in soul and pride
And it's your law, which you abide

I Wonder
by Tommy McQuaid

When I'm watching TV or doing much of nothing
That is when I begin to wonder
What destroyed towns look like
Destroyed towns are like dead people, nothing living
When I'm riding my bike that is when I begin to wonder
How big are sand dunes? Is there life in them?
I wonder what makes a strong soldier
How brave are they?
And how willing are they to fight, fighting for our freedom?
When I'm riding in my dad's car that is when I begin to wonder
Will we win this war?
I wonder if a desk job is the best job over there
I wish he were home

Surrounded
by Stephanie Motyka

Waiting in a line as far as the eye can see
The doors opened
Everyone rushed in like cattle before dinner
Floor vibrating, feeling weightless as I rush in the door
Can hardly make out the faces of the people surrounding me
They look so determined, urgent to get there before me
As if they were against me
Eyes staring at me as if I don't belong

Spring
by Victoria Murphy

Spring means
Waves of flowers
That hold the world
In peace and beauty

My Grandpa
by Sarah Marks

Joe Nagata, my grandpa
He loved his family, oh, so much
He had a bright life, from fighting in the war
To winning the Orange Bowl when he played for LSU
To just coaching football at Eunice High
He had love in his eyes, and care in his touch
He is gone, but his spirit lives on

Childhood
by Rob DiDomenico

Sitting under willows watching the butterflies fly
Childhood is a wonder that seems to flutter by
Playing in the sunshine of a summer afternoon
The joy one feels in childhood goes away far too soon
No matter how you love it, it just keeps marching past
And if you don't take advantage it will leave you fast
So enjoy it while you have it, rejoice in the average day
Don't worry about tomorrow or today will pass away

Worth It
by Regan Hire

Are real friends worth it, fighting over boys?
Although sometimes she has a fit, could this be a ploy?
Are real friends worth it, I might wonder if
Is it a bottomless pit or it might be a tiny tiff?
Are real friends worth it, shopping hand-in-hand at the mall?
Sometimes she makes me want to spit, and others make me want to bawl
Are real friends worth it, we fit together like a glove
She and I are the puzzle pieces to a kit, while, like glue, it is held together with love
Are real friends worth it, she shall always be there to call
She and I eternally commit, and will be together forever, all in all

People
by Jake Comeau

People walking by
Screaming, running, yelling
Going to work, going to school
Kids in strollers, adults on bikes
Old people sitting on benches taking in the scene before them
People scurrying about streets and sidewalks

The Tree House
by Matthew Giordano

My tree house is where I go, to pretend things are not so
It's a quiet place to be, where I see what no one else sees
One day my tree house will be a boat, and across stormy seas I will float
"Aye," the captain shouts out loud, "Set a course through this foggy cloud"
In the blizzarding days of old man winter, I scale the snow slopes of Mt. McKinter
Now I realize that I'm brave and bold
To make this journey, one doesn't have to be that old
Tomorrow night when the moon is waning
I'll hop on board for a midnight planing; high above the trees I'll fly
And soon my propellers will touch the sky
Next week my tree house will bring me back in time
And a stegosaurus I will find
I will try to bring that steggie back, but a T-Rex blocks my track
My tree house is where I go, to pretend things that are not so
So very soon you will see how much fun a tree house can be

Stormy
by Derek Desautels

I found a sexy cat
Whose lovely name was Stormy
While playing on a day
Eating, sleeping all night long
4 feet and colored black
Stormy is the cat I like

Brothers
by Patrick Sharron

Brothers
Nice, exciting
Playing, learning, teaching
Jay, Jon, Patrick, parents
Driving, going, doing
Dirty, fun
Brothers

Three Wishes
by Daniel Yong

If you had three wishes, what would they be?
Would it be for your satisfaction?
Or maybe for someone else?
Or for the world?
If I had three wishes, I would wish for my satisfaction
World peace, no terrorists, no weapons, and finally, no violence
I would wish for my family

The Cat's Eyes
by Greg Lidrbauch

Watching with those eyes
Those bright and golden eyes
The all-knowing eyes
Always watching, knowing
Knowing what, knowing where, and knowing when
These eyes can answer all questions
They are the essence of the universe

The Dentist's Office
by Chelsea Moore

Today was the scariest day
I told my mom I wouldn't go, no way!
She dragged me and pulled me, but I wouldn't budge
I was as stiff as a tree and planning a grudge
Dentist's offices are no fun
And I mean this for everyone
As I wait in my room, I can feel the pain
As if it were me on Newbury Lane
The nurse came out and pulled back her hair
I had to sit in that shiny, blue, dentist's chair
I kicked and I screamed, but they wouldn't let go
They took out their tools and I prayed no blood would show
At the sight of the shot, I was sure I passed out
And when I awoke, my teeth were all clean, like a water spout
All the kids at school lied; it's not like they're chemists
Next time I won't believe them, and go to the dentist

Remembering September
by Christopher Bell

That day in September of sorrow
Open house would have to wait until tomorrow
I was in third grade
A lot of enemies were made
It would bring the U.S.A. together
We would remember it forever
The Red, White, and Blue
In the planes, foes flew

School Days
by Nicole Bryant

Pencils, flying across paper
Markers, bringing pictures to life
Scattered papers, lying lonely on the floor
Notebooks, with work from the morning
Loud hallways, kids rushing to their next class trying to be on time
The tick tock of the clock that kids stare at all day
And yell hurray, when the bell rings at the end of the day

Squish!
by Hannah McParland

One foot in a river
One foot in the lake
What wonderful strides
A giant can take!
The water goes, "Squish"
When he wiggles his toes
Oh, giants have fun
As everyone knows
His red rubber boots
Reach up to his knees
Why, puddles are nothing
To giants like me!

When the Time Is Right
by Danielle Robbie

All the love in the air
All the love in people's heart
All the people in love holding hands
All the people in love together
All the love inside makes me sad and lonely
Only if I had someone special to keep me nice and warm on a cold night
I will find that special person when the time is right

Someone Special
by Taylor Karczewski

Someone I can trust to tell secrets to
Someone I will always be there for too
Someone who can laugh to share jokes with
Someone I can be myself around and know they won't care
Someone to love just for their hugs
Someone to go to when I need support the most
Someone I can go to when I need advice
I have a special someone
I wouldn't know what to do without them
Let's always be friends
- To all my friends

Death and Despair
by Andrew Waszak

Broken glass on the floor on the night an accident happened
No more people ever came back
Funerals came and went
Sitting in chairs, drinking tea
Uproar came in this house, people scattered in this house
Bang! And they were gone
Except one girl he never found; she had called 9-1-1
The police and ambulance came, surrounding the house with the bright lights
They went outside with their hands up high, dropped the guns with a smack
Police threw them in jail
Now it's just a faint memory
They died in jail with a death sentence
So she was safe from them, but still had worries

The Game Winner
by Kiernan O'Malley

The Red Sox and Yankees's rivalry is heated
Each game coming so close
In terms of competition and sports
This duo is viewed by most
The crowd is going crazy
A tie in the ninth so it's tight
Mariano Rivera is brought in
To end this exciting night
Manny Ramirez steps up to the plate
Not a fan in Fenway is sitting
A rude remark from a Yankee fan
But all he thinks is hitting
The first pitch is in
And ouch! A strike is called
But power-hitting Manny just shrugs it off
Keeping an eye on the ball
The second pitch is thrown
Manny steps in and hits it long
The ball is going back, way back
That ball is gone!

The Feeling of the Stage
by Lauren Dunn

You know the feeling, the feeling in your stomach that tells you, "This is it"
The feeling that everyone is watching
The feeling that everything is stopping
The feeling of people feeding on your every move
The feeling that everyone is going to see what you've accomplished
This is the feeling of the stage
Whether you're singing or dancing, acting or prancing, we all get this feeling
It's the feeling of the stage
At one point or another, now or some other, we all feel this feeling
It's the feeling of the stage

On the Beach
by Bryna Shuman

I sit
I sit on the beach
The waves splash demandingly on the sand
The sand that weaves itself into my hair
The stars sparkle in the dark sky
Twinkling, laughing, telling me to dive
To dive into the sea, but the sea is cold
The night is cold; I pick myself up
I say goodbye before going home
Home to a night of dreams
Dreams of the beach

1 Burger
by Gregory Norris

Lettuce, tomato, pickles, and cheese
A pound of ground chuck and sesame seeds
This burger tastes delicious and so very fine
That's why it's on people's plates when they dine
Everybody who's had it, said it was good
If you haven't tried it, maybe you should
When I created this burger, I didn't know what to say
Everyone who tasted it asked for seconds that day
I soon became the coolest kid in school
Because my burgers made everyone drool

Defining Dreams
by Christine Vasselin

Dreams define a way of living
Each one is different
A dream lets people live their life
If there were no dreams, where would we be?
Dreams define who we are
And how driven we are to succeed
They lead us the better and worse ways of life
Is it the joy of knowing you will be successful?
That one goal in your life not only defines you, but also your future

A Motor, a Frame, a Day of Fun
by Zach Elkins

Motor humming, gears spinning
I'm not racing, I'm not winning
Whoops, wheelies, so much fun
Engine as hot as the burning sun
Jumps, bumps, and table tops, too
I sometimes crash without a clue
I used to go slow, now I'm fast
Without my dirt bike, the fun would not last

Running Out of Time
by Kaitlin Masden

The black rusted hands of an old grandfather clock
When the sun slowly sets and the moon rises up
Every drop of sand that falls from an hourglass
Time flies on by, how long can it last?
Seconds, minutes, hours, days
So much to do with so little time
We waste it, we want it, we can't have enough
Time is like a river; it goes on forever at its own special pace
Take your time, life isn't a race

Adventure In a Night
by Emma Gifford

I climbed the highest mountain, the snow beating down on me
I swam through a river of gold, surrounded by silver leaves
I raced in a deep, dark jungle, with nothing but giant trees
I sailed to the moon and back, on silent, starry seas
I came by the valley of homework, and fought off all the lies
Until I had found treasure, and awoke with sun in my eyes

Forest Beauty
by Dylan Embry

The woods, the only place not touched by stone, metal, and the noise of the cities
Forest is the best place for quiet
And absorbing the beauty of nature's wonderful colors
And the feel of what once was
In days, the sun comes up, shining through the trees
Like a leaf covered roof with emerald green colors
The moon appears at night with a sky blue light shining through the trees
Bringing the sound of chirping crickets as beautiful as a lullaby
This quiet sanctuary is the real Heaven on Earth to me

Death's Rain
by Matt Garrity

Blood rushing from my chest
Crimson Nile from my breast
Each breath laced in pain
While in the rain
I lay and weakly I say, "To life, to death!"
To strife, to breath!"
The rain drops
The birds fly from tree tops
The ground, my final resting place
Wide and full of space
And with my near final breath
I soon accept death
My head slumps
My hand rests upon stumps
Of flower stems
This world is condemned
To eternal pain
As I sit dying in the rain

The Story of Bob
by Jack Garratt

Meet Bob, Bob doesn't have a job because he is such a slob
His teeth are more yellow than corn on the cob
Bob sleeps in a barn and smells like a farm
He eats lots of candy and doesn't look dandy
He has bad B.O. and never uses D.O.
He smells like a gym locker right after soccer
And Bob still can't figure out why he can't get a job
It's because he's a fool who dropped out of preschool

Football Keeper
by Conor Hancock

Soccer, so many positions and so many players
But there is only one position for me
Diving for balls, amazing saves, penalties blocked
These are the ways ... of a goalie
So when I put on my uniform to prepare to play
I have to be ready because I have to make saves

Pretend
by Andrea Sargent

We all pretend
Whether you pretend to be a princess or a carbon copy of the "all American"
We pretend, but we are still ourselves
We all want to be someone else, even if it is for only a moment
We refuse the accusations made; we don't want to believe it
Although we can't fight it forever, because our masks are slowly falling off
No matter how painstakingly we attempt to glue them back together
We all pretend
Sometimes because of peoples' prejudices
Or we are trying to deny the honesty and actuality of life
'Cause when you are an outcast, abandoned
The sun darkens and the moon blends in with the black canvas cradling it
And you, you are the smallest star, fading slowly
When you are rejected, all you can remember is the pain, the desperation
And the burden of their judgment sucking away like a leech across your heart
Without any regard to how precariously you try to cleanse yourself
We all pretend, but for many
It is time to discard the cloak "protecting" us from the world

Nothing To Write About
by Emma Shea

There's nothing to write about, not anything at all
I'm racking my brain, but I just can't recall
Gee, this poetry business is really dumb
I sure do wish those words would come!
I've been sitting here at this desk of mine
Wishing I could just resign
My brain's fresh out of those writing ideas I once had
Boy, this is making me really mad!
I don't like writing now, for it's making my blood boil
I feel like I'm ready to spoil
I glance up at the clock, now feeling really, truly blue
It's already quarter of two!
I feel my heart sink, and I start to get dizzy
Then I thought to myself, "I've got to get busy!"
I place my pencil towards the blank page
My feelings turning to pure rage
Then, like a light bulb popped into my head
The idea started to spread ...
I know what I can write about! It's simply very clear
I sat up straight and wiped away my tear
What I've been doing all along can surely count as writing
I never thought getting your ideas on paper could ever be exciting!
I jotted down the letters and words I have been fretting about all this time
Look, my poem even has a rhyme!
I know it is now the hour
To show my teacher that I have writing power
I waltz right into class with a grin from ear to ear, without any trace of fear
"Teacher, teacher! Look what I have here!"
"A lovely poem, I see," is all she says to me
The anticipation is growing strong
But yet, I feel that I really do belong
"Very nice, I like it a lot"
"My hard work and agony has really paid off," I thought
I like writing now that I've written a superb piece
The teacher then interrupted my daydream
"Um, excuse me; you do know there wasn't a poem due today?"
And I just stopped and exclaimed, "Oh, what the hey!"

I Can't Go To Sleep!
by Adriana Joe

I can't go to sleep, there's just too much on my mind
I don't know if it's the bully being kind ... or is it just my mind?
Last night, the girls at my sleepover gave me a fright
With all their scary stories and all their ideas, I don't know why I'm so worried
I'm so nervous about the test, but all my mom will say is, "Do your best!"
I had the scariest dream; it was me on the balance beam
Ahh, I'm so scared, about me being dared

An Ocean Deep
by Shannon Sholds

Jade waves flow over a silent ship; the sea is serene and moaning
The depths of the ocean hold secrets, stories untold and waiting to bloom
A storm begins to arise, as the bright morning sun begins to set
Rain sprinkles down and a thick, white, sea foam splashes against the rocks
Boats leave the harbor and an amazing full moon appears in the dark night sky
Sailboats toss and turn in the restless waters, as the moonlight caresses the land
Everything is quiet, and all I hear are the waves smacking against a ship's keel
The rain turns into a refreshing mist, and I believe the storm has passed
The rain has stopped
But a massive fog has begun to engulf the silhouettes of the waters
Shadows creep across the dark, mysterious sea
And the stars cast glittery lights in the murky ocean
Ships illuminate with spotlights as a lighthouse brightens the scenery

Clocks
by Zach McAuliffe

Clocks are circular, big hand, little hand
Let's not forget the tiny red hand
So many numbers all around
Hey, clock, what is the time?
What did you say, "No!"
Please I have people to see and places to go
Please, dearest clock, tell me the time
How about a give a dime?
Thank you clock
Now all you need is a dime to get the time
Well I say my farewell and goodbye my clock

Cruising Through the Sea
by Jasmine Gilpin

How I love cruising through the sea
It fills me with such glee
To see the waves dance across the ocean
Fills me with such emotion
To feel the mist on my face
Is such a simple grace

My Angel
by Jutta H. Boliver

My angel is mine, my angel on earth
My guidance to life, my reason for birth
My laughter and joy
My date with a boy
My pillow for me to cry on
My tissue to dry my eyes on
My angel to rely on, my angel is mine
My angel from above
Heaven sent; here to give me love
My angel

Mystery Balloon
by Nicole McGovern

Slow and soft, my eyes drift open
Rubbing sleep out of my eyes like rubbing sand off of paper
I move at a slow pace like a snail in a race
The sounds of tires swirl through my head
Leaping out to the car, like a frog trying to fly
The fresh, new breeze swings swiftly through my hair
Donut glaze snow covers my face
A big, cozy blanket flew over me like a wave in the sea
Hold on, hold on, hold on
My wagon whispered in my ear as we flew through the lumpy grass
The balloons blew up into a colorful rainbow against the faded light of the sunrise
The fire of a dragon roars in my face as the steam cuts cleanly through my skin
The big blown balloon rises over my head making a shadow in through the morning
Smaller and smaller, it fades away
Not knowing where it is, I kiss it goodbye until next year

Song
by Kelly Reid

I was walking along
When I started to sing a song
They danced through the streets
Those beautiful beats
They tapped on everyone's ear
And said, "Listen here
I am a beat full of sound
So stomp those feet on the ground!"
So everyone listened and danced
The ground started shaking from the people who pranced
The earth would split if I don't tell them to stop
So I held my breath so those beats would drop
I was walking along
When I wanted to sing a song
But I didn't, in fear the earth would be gone
I will never again sing a song

You Do This To Me
by Carmen Melendez

You try to help me; you say it's my choice
But throughout this conversation, I only hear your voice
You pile all this pressure, when it's my problem to solve
It was all going good till you got involved
I'm entitled to my opinion, and I don't want yours
Hello! Can't you see I can't take anymore?
Just stop with the nagging, and the "I'm just trying to help"
Well, you're not! Are you blind to see the feelings I've felt
You bring it up, and I can tell that you try
To force out the tears to make me suffer and cry
You do this to me; you make me pout and weep
To where I can't catch my breath, to where I can't go to sleep
You do this to me; you make me think that I did it
But the truth is you're not man enough to admit it
That you cause my pain and in every last tear
There's an ingredient that's made of horror and fear
All of those tears that I cry every day
In hope of maybe, you may be, just may
Stop being so harsh and let the thing go
You do this to me, just want you to know

The Lawn Gnome
by Brittney Woodrum

You might look past your average lawn gnome
But at night they begin to roam all through your home
Outside and in
Through your garbage bin
Down your halls
And up your walls
Under your rugs
And even in your coffee mugs
Opening your refrigerator door
Leaving only an apple core
But as soon as the lights come on
They dash back blending in with your lawn

Killer Pinecone
by Eric Soule

An innocent pinecone sitting in a tree
Falls down and kills somebody
No one knew, no one knows
But the guy who got killed doesn't like pinecones
Alas a teeny, tiny thing
It brings great pain and wondering
What had happened, when and where?
It turns out it fell from the air

Do You Know
by Alyssa Glover

Everyday I see your face
When you walk by I'm looking at your sparkling eyes and your great smile
Looking back to see if you're looking at me, trying to impress you everyday
Even when I am playing basketball, I'm trying to look cute
And trying to get your attention, flirting with you all day long
When we hang out, I love it when you make me smile
Calling you just to hear your voice
Thinking about you all day long and can't get you out of my mind
Wishing we could be together everyday, but something is in the way

No Turning Back
by Davidson Louissaint

There is no way to see what's behind and ahead of me
And on my mind are the great dangers that can pop-up
Is a thirteen-year-old supposed to be scared of things?
If not, then why am I? Why am I scared?
I can tell that unexpected things may pop-up if I'm not observant
I must find a solution to get out of this place; I am scared
There's no one here except me
I don't think there is someone even 6 miles from here that can help
I turn left and right every other second, waiting until I see someone
Night and day I pray for somebody to come
I pray somebody would rescue me from this unsafe place
One week's gone by, two weeks are gone by; no one in sight so far
Some mysterious person is approaching me
He is getting closer and closer by the second
He approached me with a weird looking face
He said, "Are you ok? You look afraid"
I asked him if he could guide me back to where I came from
In a deep voice he said that there was no turning back from this point
"No turning back," I said to myself, I am going to have to deal with it

Nature
by Jake Andre

Nature can be found everywhere
The wind whispering through the leaves
Branches bending on the tall willow trees
The cave in which lives a bear
In the winter, the tree branches which are bare
The fireflies you may see on midsummer eves
The spider, whose delicate web it will weave
Nature can be found anywhere
It may be in a cave
As nature flashes by unnoticed
The dirt that covers someone's grave
Nature flashes by unnoticed
On the beach, a crashing wave
Nature flashes by unnoticed

The Out
by Ryan Benoit

The bright yellow sun
Blazing on our dark maroon caps, gave amazing heat to make us sweat
We were in the last inning and about to win the championship
Digging my cleats into the dry dirt, ready for the ball to come to me
Screams and cheers are coming from the stands
There are two outs already, and the next batter coming to the plate
The first pitch was going right down the middle of the plate
And all of a sudden like thunder striking, a loud ping, a hard drive over my head
The right fielder got it and threw the ball hard to first base
Everyone waiting for it, growing anxiety, and there it was
The umpire screamed, "Out!"
Everyone cheered happily!

Writing
by Deirdre Harnett

My hand writes, I have no control, my hand floats
My pen writes, my mind thinks, my mouth moves
My grip is strong, so the pen won't slip; I have no time to erase
My mind doesn't like this poem, but my hand won't stop
My hand tells me that this is my moment, and not to let it slip
My mind says that there is always tomorrow, but my hand says, "Now!"

Present
by Ken Ramos

Here are some types of sweets
I like to put in my mouth
Laffy Taffy, Starburst, Milky Way
Jolly Ranchers, Shock Tarts
Here are some sweets
I don't like in my mouth
Pay Day, Reese's, Peanut M&M's
Baby Ruth's, Lemon Heads
So next time you're going to buy me a present
Make sure it's not candy I hate

My Big, Old Dog
by Jesenia Santiago

My big old dog has lost her puppies
And doesn't know where to find them
She goes down the street to look everywhere to find them

Explosions
by Matt MacDonald

Bombs can kill people
Explosions can destroy all
That car is bombing

Goalie
by Jacob Ullom

I can see, cool, cut shavings of snow
On a thick blanket of ice
My sharp, wet blades scraping the frozen water
Sliding like a penguin on its belly
In the net, stopping black, round disks
Having the time of my life in the net

September
by Patrick Ciapciak

When the first day of school begins
And the leaves outside begin to change
And the football season begins
And the farmer starts his harvest
When bees are singing their late summer song
Then you know it's September
When the cooler temperatures overcome
And the sky shows more stars than before
And air-conditioning is turned to heat
And the landscape a fiery tie-dye
When the crops are picked one last time
Then you know it's September

True Love Hurts
by Callie Campbell

I can't explain what I see in your eyes
When I look in your eyes, I get butterflies
When I see you, you're all that matters
But when you're gone, my heart shatters
I want to tell you how I feel
So we can make our love real
You are my whole heart
So promise me we will never part
You know that we are meant for each other
But I don't want to be like your others
But now, since you did me wrong
We're not getting along
I wish you still loved me
As much as I still love you
But now I've realized
That our true love hurts

Treasure Map
by Dillon Crosby

Over a hill, under a bridge
Go north till you get a chill, next look in the fridge
Behind the moldy cheese, past the old milk
Push your head in till it starts to freeze, and you will find some silk
Don't ask me why, but it is there
You can throw it into the air, but don't forget to share!

'Twas the Day After Christmas
by Alex Robke

'Twas the day after Christmas and all through the room
Paper and broken toys are haphazardly strewn
Everybody is mad, all their patience spent
They are tired of the fruitcake their relatives sent
They send cheap little cards wishing good will and health
And all they money they have, they just spend on themselves
The true meaning of Christmas is forgotten quite quickly
Kids feasting on candy canes, turn green and look sickly
Yes, Christmas is over and chaos does thrive
Happy New Year to all ... I hope you survive

Stranded
by Samuel Pereira

Stranded on an island waiting for the call
Under our shelter, we hear the raindrops fall
Water drips down all of the walls
This is very depressing for us all
Drip, drip, drip; drop, drop, drop
When will this rain ever stop?
We are not able to grow any crops
We're stranded on an island; we can't go shop
If we don't leave now, I'm going to blow
I really, really, really, want to go
Actually, it's starting to show
Time is going by way too slow

Crows
by Mikayla Michienzi

Crows are black storm clouds against the silhouetted blue sky
Like a train's whistle, they cry
As they fly across the blue sky

Soldiers
by Jazzmine Rabe

Soldiers die, Americans cry
Family members scream, why Lord? Why?
The price of freedom is death
Our patriots and our deceased soldiers are the best
They risk their lives just to save ours
Some come home with cuts and scars
Some come home in coffins
Some are captured like our dear Matt Maupin
Some are being tortured; some are being bombed
I feel bad for grandparents, dads and moms
I wish this war would stop; I wish this thing would end
I wish we could stop fighting; I wish we could be friends
So many lives lost, so many tears have fallen
Outside I keep a happy face, but inside I want to yell

Freedom
by Alicia Mahoney

The sun may be gone, the hope may be faded, but still a little remains
We must have faith; the imagination of peace is near
That's why we need to accomplish this deed
For every person who wants to be free
For every child who wants to see the stars on the flag
Shine bright through the mist, the day, and starry night
For the flag waving proud and strong in the wind
For all who have come so far to make this country what it is today; great
This is the country everyone wants to go to
The country of hope, bravery, and freedom
We fight for that little hope of peace
We fight for the day we will see the sun shine again
And it will shine all the more, better and brighter
We fight for freedom

My Aunt, Gail
by Matthew Felch

You love me, and I love you, too
You've been there for me, now I'm there for you
I'm with you, so is God also
With him you're safe, I know, I know
You need us now, more than ever
You'll pull through, just never say never
Get well soon, I know you'll pull through
Because I'm right here, and God is, too

Never-Ending Road
by Katherine Dennis

Friendship is a never-ending road
There is no destination, but a promise
Hand in hand we walk this road, finding bits of ourselves along the way
Through obstacles we roam, get stuck sometimes, but we make it through
Have our best times, and worst, together
Help each other when we fall, pull us up when we are down
More people may join, but we're always there
Struggling past other people, trying to make it on our own
Things may not always be perfect, maybe no fairy tale ending
But for now, at least, we're happy ever after

Rose
by Jeffrey Romano

So wonderfully red, and the stem with thorns
You stick out like a bull's horns
An exquisite flower, will never see doom
You glisten in the night like the beautiful moon
You stick out from all the rest, like a polka-dotted house
You can be big or small, like a dog or a mouse
You are the queen of the garden, you have no foes
You are the most beautiful, you delicate rose

My Guardian Angel
by Alexandra Halley

Did you ever feel that you love someone so much that
You would do anything just so that they could stay alive?
Well, I felt that way!
Not just anyone died, my great grandfather, my papa, my guardian angel
The one person who would do anything and bend over backwards just for me
Now he's in a happier place called Heaven
Rest in peace Papa, I will always love and remember you

Please, Daddy
by Rachel Shaughnessey

Girls are always asking for things in, "Please, Daddy"
If they want something it's, "Please, Daddy," he doesn't even need to say, "No"
Please, can I have a pony?
Please, can we get a dog, Daddy?
Please, can we live on a lake?
He just gives the eyes of, "No"
But as you get older, the "Please, Daddy's," get less ridiculous
They become important questions, but they never have the answer in words
Please, Daddy, meet your son-in-law
Please, Daddy, walk me down the aisle?
Please, Daddy, meet your grandson?
Please, Daddy, come to dinner?
This time he doesn't answer immediately, he just looks at me
He gives me the eyes, except they're different
They are eyes of, "Yes," tears, and happiness!

Nantucket
by Taylor Grey

The little, grey island out in the sea
Too far out for anyone to see
Shrouded in fog like a smoky bog
Sand filled shoes are easy to lose
In the town near the bay
Where many small boats lay
Along the roads
The daffodils sing a yellow melody
On Altar Rock where the hawks prey
The sandy mazes of roads wither and wind
I'm very fond of Hummock's pond
At the beach where best friends bond
The little, grey island out in the sea
Too far out for anyone to see

This Is the End
by Chelsey Henderson

Down the path of darkness
We have been betrayed
My flesh is growing warmer
I know this is the end
As cold chills race through my spine
I feel the dampness in the air
My destiny lies before me
I know this is the end
The air is thick with the ashes of disfigured corpses
As I approach this bottomless pit
I feel as if I'm walking straight into hell itself
I know this is the end
The flames are tickling my flesh
Death is dancing all around
The fire is laughing now
I know this is the end
As I am pushed into the fire
I say one last prayer
As the flame devours my flesh
I know this truly is the end

Iraq
by Alyssa Copelas

Lyin' in my bed, wonderin' when they'll come home
The war goes on, but the soldiers still roam
Listenin' to all the radio reports but tryin' to cope
Families cry but don't lose hope
That soon the war will end, and they can once again see the ones
That worked so hard to stop all the guns
Not knowin' if they'll ever see the world the same
All the soldiers protecting people in their hidden fame
They stare into the sky and hope
That God will help them cope

I'll Be Right Here
by Kimberly Fears

When the Earth begins to shake and the ground begins to quake
If they see you and can feel, all the confidence to take
I'll be right here holding you down
If the sky should suddenly fall, and crumble the mountains tall
As the air begins to thin and you cannot breathe at all
I'll be right here to shield you and give you air
If your path should fade away, and a brick wall should cause delay
If you're just too weak to knock it down and you can't wait another day
I'll be right here to demolish it and clear your path
For I am your friend, your pair of wings, I'll give you joy and the comfort it brings
And when our days are over and your heart no longer sings
I'll be right here to open the gates, right here to open the gates

Spring
by Sarah Robinson

Shining sun, warm day
Green grass and a picnic lunch
All my family gathered around me
Uncle Bennett and Aunt Suzy, cousins, Christian and Elliot
Vacation ends, school begins
Shining sun into your classroom
Highlights the whiteboard
Birds singing, children playing, dirty brown hands
A new life
A new beginning

Winter
by Bram Daly

Winter, it's winter, wonderful winter!
With snowballs flying everywhere
Winter, it's winter, wonderful winter!
With kids making snowmen for the holiday
Winter, it's winter, wonderful winter!
With kids and men alike sledding down the hill
Winter, it's winter, wonderful winter!
Time to go skiing with tons of fun
Winter, it's winter, wonderful winter!
Watching the Olympics, do lots of tricks
Winter, it's winter, wonderful winter!
Running inside because hot chocolate is ready
Winter, it's winter, wonderful winter!
The snow is turning to mush
Winter, it's winter, wonderful winter!
Wait! It's not winter, it's spring!

As the Wind Blows
by Gabrielle Rennolds

As the wind blows through my hair
I see the sun with a beautiful glare
Soon the birds will fly away
And the squirrels will come and play
Then I hear a bee with a buzz
While a ladybug does what it does
Again I hear the wind come by
And so again, the trees will cry
The pines are falling to the ground
Then they'll fall without a sound
Soon comes by a family
Until I see another bee
In my arm, where I felt the sting
The wind became my healing wing
Now the sun falls to end the day
But the sun has left without a say
The wind will now blow, so very soon
And soon it will bring the midnight moon
As the wind blows through my hair
I see the moon, with that midnight glare

A Look On the Inside
by Anita Sodder

Beyond the long eyelashes is a girl full of dreams
A kooky girl, an entertaining girl; an outgoing, hilarious, drama queen
Beyond the tan skin is a Fruit Loop surrounded by the Cheerios of the world
Awaiting her moment to shine, behind the dazzling brown eyes
Is a shopaholic, a scrap booker, and a dancer showing off her talents to all
Behind the thick hair, is a Christian who knows God made her beautiful
A person knowing God is with her always
Beside the curvy body is a messy family
People loving all of its members, each in their own special way
Beside the brace-face are amazing, fabulous, outgoing friends
Sticking together, enjoying their life, being themselves
Standing right in front of you is Anita Sodder, a special someone for who she is
Herself

God Bless Them ... One and All
by Allison Levy

Wars are horrible; we watch them on the news
We see them first hand; it scares us
Seeing them is bad ... what about living through them?
Everyday, both women and men, all colors, all religions, all different
Come together as one to defend this country that so many of us call home
Blood is shed, the innocent lose their lives; families lose loved ones
Lives are taken as quickly as a gun can be fired
All to defend the Red, White, and Blue
We should all do our part, help out as best we can
We are not reminded daily of all the horrors of war
Some of our fellow Americans are
Some people lose their lives, others lose loved ones
Some people lose their best friends
The people at home just lose interest after the first commercial on Channel 4
We should always remember all who serve this country
One day a year, November 11th to be exact
We should all really show our part in defending this country
One day a year? Try 365
Respect Veterans Day, forever and always
Respect those who defend the Red, White, and Blue
God bless them, one and all

Lynx
by Kimberly Steen

In the dry, forsaken lands
Of dunes of gold and dusty sands
There on prowl, the warrior stands
Closer to his prey, he nears
Sleeking back his tufted ears
Moments away from his victim's worst fears
And in the dust and dirt he lays
With claws of death to kill his prey
To him this is but mere child's play
And with a deadly, murderous skill
Like lightning, he dives upon his kill
Completing one more deadly drill

Ducks
by Thomas Lucchini

I tease two ducks
Jumping blue ducks washing jumping yellow ducks
Creepy I hear tiny ducks shrinking
Please taste blue ducks
I taste blue ducks
Creepy I tasted gray ducks

Special Friend
by Sabrina Staras

You are beautiful on the inside and out
You always know what to say without a doubt
When I'm struggling to make the right choice
Judgment or criticism won't be in your voice
While I'm down with defeat
Seeing you is a treat
Why you are my special friend, a friend that is true
A friend that doesn't just last a day or two
You're not afraid to compliment
When I'm down you stop the torment
Yes you are my special friend
And I will never trade you in because you are my special friend
Until the very end

Untitled
by Gabby LaFalam

The road stretches farther
Will I make it in these chilling winds?
The trees are merely a blur that follow the cracked, fading tar
Will this road ever mend?
The freezing wind pierces my face as the blanket of white covers the forest floor
What is to come around the next corner?
Trees sway to the rhythmic whistle of the wind
The sounds of faded wind chimes in the distance form a duet
Will this soothing sensation last?
The sun shines through the trees lighting the way
Will I ever reach the end?!
The chimes die down as the wind softens into a tranquil breeze
The trees become visible
I approach a heavenly figure that glistens in the sun
"I am here to guide you. You are given a question, just one"
With no hesitation I reply, "Do you perhaps have a map you could lend?"
"My child, there is no need for a map, for I haven't one to lend
But you my dear, are pacing down a road that has no end"

The Hero of the Game
by Shane Rider

Sports, they're great fun
In baseball, the pitcher is the king of the field
He controls the action, the speed, the drama
As he winds up and throws, it could make or break the game
The devotion, dedication, is lost as the batter becomes the hero

A Bad Day
by Ryan Trainor

Teacher yelling, yelling hard
Wet outside, dogs are sad
Birds dying, birds not flying
Books are stolen, students fighting
Gross food, no one eats
A car crashes
Clouds over the sun, misty atmosphere

A Wonderful Fourth of July
by Rachel Wilson

When I saw the first fireworks, I knew it was going to be a wonderful Fourth of July
I was amazed when I saw gorgeous colors dancing in the moonlit sky
Hazy smoke floating through the dusky air
Content faces of people staring into the sky
My ears heard roaring noises booming like thunder in a storm
Young children sobbing in fright, bright rockets whistling like a fall breeze
My body felt the booms and cracks, making my tight chest pound rapidly
The solid ground shaking like an earthquake
The moist sweat dripping down my face
My nose tingled when I smelled strong smoke from the fireworks
Burning like a campfire
The scent of buttery popcorn, popping in the scorching kettle
Sweet, fluffy cotton candy drifting through the air
My mouth watered when I tasted red watermelon that was dripping onto my lap
Caramel apples oozing like a volcano, crisp apple pie cooling on a table close by
On this hot, summer Fourth of July evening
All of my senses experience the sights, sounds, feelings, smells, and tastes
Of this exciting holiday festival

Rush
by Samantha Harrison

Rushing on the court, rushing to my post; server on the left court
Tweet, the whistle blows from the referee tower, her hand gestures ready
Rush of energy shouting through my body, like a needle that had just been injected
Rushing my arm, swing back and smack
The ball goes flying over the net, dashing over the net
The next rush of excitement comes as the ball hit the court
I hit it with all my might
No one dares to try to interfere with a ball moving that fast
The rush again and again, six times in a row
Now rotating to the second biggest job on the court
It flies over and is returned, that I would be feeling if I did not
Embarrassment is what I thought if I had not lifted that ball enough
Everyone would yell and shout; the ball is soaring over the net towards me
Hurry up and wait, an old trick my coach taught me
A rush of energy hit me
And I smacked the ball just hard enough to lift it over the net
No attempt to go after it
Rushing of excitement like a lightning bolt striking a metal object
We won!

Maybelle Ann
by Haley McGough

Search the whole ocean and perhaps you can
Catch a rare glimpse of Maybelle Ann
And her ship made entirely of silver and gold
Or even the chest where her money is shoaled
She'd bombard the ship with cannonballs plenty
And take aboard her scallywags twenty
To go through such extensive measures
And search the ship for all the treasures
She was busy sailing the oceans
While in her flask there was slipped a potion
Which made her dizzy and in a state
And she fell in love with her own first mate
And so they began as a pair
But one thought, "How would others' fare?"
If we told the rest of the clan
Of the love of Maybelle Ann
Then tragic actions set them apart
They found his own sword plunged through his heart
So chained to her chest and grasping his sword
Maybelle Ann jumped overboard

Believing
by Kaitlin Pupa

Some days, when I look up at the sky
The sun shining and the clouds going by
I think of what tomorrow will bring
What would happen if I went to a place?
A place where no one, nor I, have ever been
And never came back?
There would be different surroundings from where I live now
New creatures, new figures, flowers for that how
People would be singing from street to street
No war would be happening, no one even on their feet
Everyone was different, one of a kind
People were saying "Hello" and not "Goodbye"
Could this mean there was no end?
Not even to a thing
I guess we will just have to wait
Until that perfect day, and see

Love's Curse and Blessing
by Vannak Khin

I wish to no longer love
The aftermath of such is cursed
Why should I feel guilt
Because my heart has tilt
Toward a maiden as fair as a dove
And my mixed feelings to her have emerged?
Oh Eros in your virtuous light
Must you burden me with these emotions?
To her of love and hate
And to my heart an open gate?
Should I pinion her from the fright
Less she see my love as a commotion?
But alas my love is to that maiden
For she makes me soar through the air
Laughing and smiling makes a trace
Of my love for her in any place!
Yet heed my warning for her heart's haven
Is to another, for life will snare
To those who can't find love to share

Sisters For Eternity
by Beth McConnell

Deaths can destroy or build a family
However, one death built a family for me
When death called my third cousin's dad
Little did we know that her life would become sad
Through it all, we will always be sisters for eternity
My cousin and I have been very close since birth
Since we have been on this beautiful Earth
We became closer at the ages of six and three
Together we formed a brand new family
Through it all, we will always be sisters for eternity
Scars from the painful past
Will forever and always last
Though, I always try to hide and lie
Though she always questions why
Through it all, we will always be sisters for eternity

Leaves
by Orren Anderson

Shhhh!
Csssss!
Living lifting leaves
Laughing lounging leaves
Speedy bullets racing down the street
Like jets flying through the clear cold air
Almost like a bird skimming the ground
Like frogs skipping and sailing down the road
They skim the ground at the speed of light
They skip around for longer than life
How far can they go ...?

Friends
by Taylor Johnson

I have many, I have few
I have best, I have just
I have girls, I have boys
I have special, I have ordinary
I have friends

Why Am I Still Awake?
by Christina Catanzaro

It's 3:00 in the morning, why am I still awake?
My eyes are dry and itchy; I'm crazy for goodness sake
I've written four poems already, that's a record for me, I'm sure
My mind is beginning to wander; I'm feeling a bit insecure
I'm at the point where I giggle and I just can't make it stop
Even if nothing is funny, the giggling I can't seem to drop
I flip through the channels, but there's nothing good on
Just stupid infomercials that are making me yawn
My mind is running away like the sea runs from the shore
There's a light at the end of the tunnel, but someone just closed the door!
Now I cannot reach my destination, the meadow of daisy land
If I can navigate away from the darkened path
Maybe I can get half the sleep I planned

Chocolate Cookie
by Emily Snell

I'm chewy
And I'm chocolaty
I'm crispy
And I'm warm
And when you start to smell me
People come running in a swarm
I come in many flavors
As many as can be
So why don't you stop by sometime
And have a plate of me?

Me
by Kinsey Hisle

In school everyone would always ask, "When you grow up what do you want to be?"
I would always answer, "I don't know! Leave me be!"
The question then went around
I couldn't help overhearing the answers sound
"When I grow up, I'm going to be a teacher!"
"Really? I'm going to become a preacher!"
So the answers went on till all of those many questioning eyes were looking at me
Then one boy asked, "Well, what is your answer going to be?"
When my answer was silence, they left me alone
I finally went back to my ice cream cone
When all of them were grown up, they found out the answer, it didn't take long
The found out what they thought they wanted to be was wrong
I was the only correct one, you see
Back then when I grew up, I only wanted to be me

A Good Game
by Jack Matthews

Begin with bags full of graphics
This will make the game fast and beautiful
Then add a cup of hard-drive; then add a cup of sound
Next, stir in some controls
Next, pour it into a CD mold, then bake for four hours
Then serve with a mouse, keyboard, CPU and a monitor
Then enjoy your game

At Gymnastics
by Alicia Parent

Classes giggling delightfully
Spring floors bouncing like beach balls, beams wobbling back and forth
Humming fans cooling us off, floor music playing for the gymnasts
Tumbling gymnasts touching the sky
Ghost-shaped chalk figures on the back of our leotards
The floor shaking beneath my feet, feeling like they hit the street
The beam squealing, "Ouch!" when you jump on it
My heart pounding hard, hands aching from rips
Dirty, disgusting socks around me, chalk dust dancing in the air
Lips rough and chapped, sweat dripping down my face
Gymnasts work hard, gymnasts work hard

Peaceful Place
by John Albani

My peaceful place is full of trees and rocks
My friends live there, such as the fox
I like to play down by the pond
The woods and I share a special bond
The sun sets down and the day is gone
Then comes the morning dawn
The fun we had is soon to end
The games we played were just pretend
Then they come to take it down
The trucks and saws come in from town
They come in here to attack
But all I want is my land back

The Storm
by Jacob Clark

The clouds are drooping like they're getting ready to explode
Some trees look very sad because they're drooping so low
The grass looks frustrated 'cause it's moving so fast
I feel nervous, then I hear a big blast
I hide underneath my bed, feeling very scared
It's now decreasing, fears start to melt away
I hoped I was dreaming, reality held fast
The details were apparent, the wind lingering and glistens
Playing like a whisper, so soft, like a harp
That puts me to sleep

A Soccer Player's Nightmare
by Alexandria Wasson

She was tearing down the field; all the girl could see was net
Not noticing me standing there, my heart filled with regret
She whizzed past the defense; I was scared, I couldn't lie
She gave that ball a mighty kick, it soared across the sky!
The crowd was standing on their feet
I heard screaming, shouting and cheers
The ball was flying too high to catch, unleashing my worst fears
But worst of all, they were L.F.C., our rival team
They were big and fast, hard to outlast, and very, very mean
I jumped in the air, sort of hung there
Touched the ball with my fingertips
It bounced off the frame, then back down it came
Suddenly, I lost my grip
Cheers came from most, jeers came from the rest
I hung my head down in shame
I work up with a scream, saw that it was just a dream, and realized we lost the game

Spring
by Jelisa Vasquez O'Hara

Spring
As I walk, I feel the wind blow through my hair
The sun shining, the birds chirping, the leaves blossoming on the trees
The feeling of spring is so nice, here sitting on the bench
My thoughts start exploring; I begin to realize things, the lake, the trees, the people
I started realizing things I would have never thought were beautiful before
And now that I thought about it, it was all so beautiful
As I looked to my right, I saw a lady jogging
She looked so graceful; as she slowed down I heard her start singing
And again I felt the presence of spring, and maybe even summer
I suddenly felt a force bring me down, but I caught myself
And when I looked down, I saw my shoelaces were untied
As I got up, I saw a dog; the look of him running made me feel warm inside
He looked so happy to be running in freedom
The cars were making a noise that caught my ear, the atmosphere was great
The wind died down and then rustled again
From where I was sitting, all the houses looked so homey
Each of them had their own design, their own way of expressing themselves
It was a nice feeling, and now looking at the sky, I could see the clouds coming
But the sky still kept its same color, and somehow still kept its same peaceful look

The White Dress
by Sylvia Meredith

Winter softly spreads her long snow-white dress across the lovely land
She makes such a beautiful sight, that is amazingly grand!
The White Dress
She has a breath that is icy cold
Children enjoy sitting in by the warm fire as Christmas stories are told!
The White Dress
Her long white dress sparkles and shines
It is so lovely that it is utterly divine!
The White Dress
The children are excited and ready to play
With winter here it is sledding, snowmen and hot chocolate all day!!
The White Dress
The children quickly grab their sleds and on goes little Ned
Mom has him bundled up from his toes to head!
The White Dress
Spring will soon come and the winter will go
The children will say goodbye to the long white dress
That was made by the fresh fallen snow!
The White Dress

Orphan Annie
by Kelsey Ford

She was a lonely little child with no place to call home
All she wanted was parents of her own
As she laid down at night to sleep
She always turned her head to weep
"Dear God, won't you please help me find some parents," said she
"I know there's someone out there for me
I don't want to go through this world alone"
When she looked at a child with a smile on their face
Everybody wondered why she felt so out of place
"It's not because I'm not loved
It's just that I need help from above"
She cried in a voice very low, "I'm a very lonely little girl
I know there's someone in this world that will give me a home of my own
Then I won't be a sad, little girl all alone"

What Does Inspiration Mean?
by Nicole Collette

An inspiration can be found at home
Perhaps a mother's welcoming arms
Greeting you like you have been gone for centuries
How about a neighbor
Nice enough to make you something sweet
For the walk back home
Maybe a teacher
Giving you the ride of a lifetime
Kind enough to keep your seat belt fastened
What about a friend
Making sure they catch you
No matter how heavy you are

My Love
by Ashley Silver

You creep into my dreams
I feel you in my heart
No matter where we are
We'll never be apart

My Mom
by Amiejanice Mendez

My mom is special to me
She is as special as can be
She keeps a clean, cozy home
We can't keep it clean when we're alone
She has a good sense of style
On display, as she strolled down the aisle
She's also a really great cook
She doesn't need instructions from the book
My friends say she's really nice
I would agree, not once, but twice
She buys me awesome clothes
Even rings for my toes
I will love her always
Even when she's old, and roaming down hallways

Bahaman Man
by Emil Bender

There was a man from the Bahamas
He fished in his pajamas
Well since he was a hack
He only caught a jack
One day he caught a skate
That day he almost met his fate
The skate was so big it pulled him into the water
To his surprise the water was much hotter
The skate pulled him till he could see no land
Trapped out at sea with his pruned hand
He did not find land for 6 hours
When he did the island was full of flowers
The island was very beautiful but small
When you come upon a small island
In the Caribbean don't be surprised to see
A man in pajamas

Fog
by Anna Kenyon

A dark grey stratus cloud sinks slowly to the ground
It is coming near
Soon fog will be here
You can feel a light mist on the back of your coat
Soon fog will be in your hair
Up your sleeves, and down your throat
Now fog is finally here
I hope the sun will soon appear

Summer Days
by James Estes

Oh, how great these summer days are, staying out till the sun goes away
Oh, so much fun it has been so far, I wish these days were here to stay
With the sun shining oh, so brightly
As if everyday was like a dream, living my life oh, so lightly
Going down to the park to get some ice cream
Playing catch with the guys till late at night
Coming home to mom all dirtied up, looking like I had been in a fight
Everything feels like one big faze
Oh, how much I love these summer days

I Love You
by Eliza Bouchard

I love you like the flowers love to glisten in the sun
Like the fish's scales shine to the night
Like the sun and the moon's affair to the sky
Like the little daffodils sitting in the garden
I love you like the stars love the moon
Like the chimney eats the smoke
I love you like the tomatoes bask in the sunlight
Like the tree roots hug the ground
Like the squirrel, eating his seeds in the moonlight
I love you like the whale loves the waves
Like a walrus loves his sleep
I love you like my lungs love air
Like my stomach loves food
Like my brain's desire for knowledge
I love you like I've never loved before
From the bottom of my heart
I love you

The Uninvited Guest
by Josh King

Without an invitation, she came
With no one in particular to blame
She's raging into shore
Gaining power more 'n' more
She was packed with fierceness and persistence
You could definitely see her in the distance
In denial, the people chose to stay
Even though danger was heading their way
Because they had survived so many others
They chose to stay with their sisters and brothers
Not realizing that the levees were so weak
They didn't know their future was so bleak
Like a thief in the night
The hurricane gusted into smite
The party city of New Orleans
Now is one of the many shattered scenes
The people can find no rest
Because of this uninvited guest

Stuffed Scarecrows
by Kristian Marzotto

Millions of critters getting scared
Scary stuffed, stealing souls
Like a stuffed grim reaper
Evil businessmen on poles
Shhhhhhhh!
As his pumpkin head jets, chuckling as it flies
Ahhh haa haa haaaaaaaa!
Killing kind critters
Unmerciful as death itself
Until next year ...

New Hampshire
by Taylor Donovan

There is a place I like to go
Especially when there is lots of snow
Snowmobiling, sledding, or building a snowman
Are some of the things my family likes to plan
Spring is nice
When there is no more ice
Taking long walks on the railroad tracks
Or through the woods to see animal tracks
Summer is fun, in the sun we bake
And going for a cool swim at Mirror Lake
Fall is beautiful with its colorful leaves
While birdies are storing their precious seeds
No city noise, no traffic jams, no ringing phone
Thornton, New Hampshire, is just like home

The Red Sox Opening Game
by Charles Lutts

Yesterday was the Red Sox's opening game
The other team played pretty lame
Ortiz hit a homer to the right
The ball hit hard, went out of sight
Coco Crisp got a finger hurt
The pitcher was Josh Beckett, it wasn't Curt
In the end we won, three to five
Another day, we made it alive

The Last Stare
by Lauren Belke

I looked at you, you looked at me
I wanted to be with you, why can't you see?
I stared at you, you looked away
Sun shining on your pure soft face
You're sitting in the perfect place
I always help you with things and such
Reading, homework, then you blush
But that is gone now, you just left me
I miss you, please come back to me
I guess I just had my last stare
Why did you leave me?
I still have some pictures, memories of you
Don't forget my face; I will miss you

Snow
by Dacia Beans

A white fluffy blanket covers the green
I hear little kids scream, scream, scream
While they laugh and play all day
I stay inside and bake away
The kids play all night and day
Because they think they are going to have a snow day
I make cookies and hot cocoa
For when they come in they are acting loco!

Bad Day
by Michelle Finnell

I got a new haircut, now I look like a nut
I wore a hat and slipped on a mat
I walked home all alone
I see a cloud, people are loud
It starts to rain, man it is a pain
I arrive at my house, not even a mouse
Is waiting for me, I go under a tree
In the distance I see a car; I can't see it is too far
My mom pulls up, I say, "What's up"
This is a bad day I really have to say

Summer Days
by Colin Driver

Summer is long
Like a four-minute song
Summer is hot
Like a boiling cooking pot
Summer is fun
When you get to run in the sun
Summer is great
While watching people skate
You will swim
Until you're slim (splish, splash)
When you run you will sweat
Like you're losing an important bet
When you are finished playing
You can laugh at all the funny jokes
But be careful not to choke
After all the jokes
Grab a glass of lemonade
And make your summer an oasis in the shade

Memories of You
by Bambi Steffey

If I could have had one last laugh, it would have been the best laugh
If I could have been there to get one last hug right before you went away
If I could have heard you say, "I love you, Dawn"
Maybe remembering you as you were is best
Cancer changes all lives
These mean more than words can ever say
You believed in me when no one else did
You encouraged me to pursue my dreams
You helped me to reach my goals
I will miss the "hammer-headed aardvark"
I love the peculiar doll you gave me
It was supposed to have been a joke; it was never funny to me
I know I can never bring you back
However, I do want you to know
My life will never be the same without you
I love you and miss you, Uncle Leon
And I will for the rest of my life

Z 50
by Homer Miller

Climbing on, ready to ride, wrist pumping to throttle
I ride the Z 50 Honda all day long
Pop! Pop! Pow!
The whining sound of tires screech on the black top
Bitter sweat rolls down my face
Under the helmet it's a hundred degrees
As I smack watermelon bubble gum
Gassy exhaust fumes spread through the air
The smooth gel-like grip of hand grips softens the vibrations
As I ride wheelies all day long
It's just like sitting on a washing machine

The Sky
by Cade Larrabee

A hawk cries
As the sun soars high
I'll always wish
I could fly into that cloudy abyss

A Day of Shopping
by Margaret Maloney

I was in the store of Coach
As I realized I forgot to call my folks
I called my parents on my cell
To make sure that all is well
As I walked into Gucci
I realized I forgot my Pucci
And much to my delight
I found out that the store was open till the wee hours of the night
As I walked into Juicy
I then saw my friend Lucy
She was purchasing a sweat suit of the color pink
And then noticed it had some fur mink
I was in Chanel
As I bumped into my dear friend Danielle
I went to say hey
But she was gone for the day

Beside His Grave
by Jordan Estep

Beside his grave
A mountain in front of my house
This is where Papaw and I used to sit and talk before he passed away
I come here to think or calm down from the day's anger
Beside his grave, white and yellow daisies reach for the sun
Red-breasted robins rest on the chain link fence chirping and singing
Ground squirrels with white stripes play tag
Beside his grave, a crystal clear stream runs down the mountain
Like a giant water fountain
The air is fresh and clear, moist grass tickles my legs as I rest
Beside his grave

My Weakness
by A.K. Olsen

There is something I must conceal
Yet it's the same thing I must reveal
It has tied me
And tried me
I have jailed myself within it well
Locking myself inside my own black cell
I could not scare it
Nor bear it
It stood somewhere inside the haze
But still it pierced me with a cold hard gaze
It has mangled me
Entangled me
And when I thought I could take it no more
Jesus said, "You have but to open the door"
I leaped out of my night
Into the light
Then I turned, looked Fear dead in the eye
The question burned in my throat, so I asked, "Why?"
Fear sneered
And he jeered
"You no longer have me," I plainly said
And in humiliation, Fear's face turned Hot Rod red
He wailed aloud
But then he bowed
Jesus forgave me for being so wrong
We both glanced at Fear and said, "So long"

Tribute To Laura
by Lucy McGowan

Laura is the most outrageous person I know
She is the director of a show
She loves to act, sing, and dance
She sometimes wears brightly colored pants
Laura is protective of her son
She won't let him alone in the sun
She named him Phineus
She wouldn't let him take the bus
I've been in four of Laura's productions so far
In one I had to fall out of a car
In Laura shows we sometimes get a topic
Because of Laura's love of gossip!

Dragons
by Winston Davey

Dragons, dragons, flying on wings of red, invited they are, one and all
The dragons are large, dragons are small, are all flying to war
Families of dragons have been invited, some of whom are excited
The raging fire will meet them and welcome them to the dragon war
Leprechauns are crafting dragon armor, pixies will don the armor
The armor, a most special gift from the god of war
The trolls will sing and dance, of wars come and gone
All dressed in black, the curtain of death arriving
All to fight with them to the end, with musicians singing songs of war
I will be the master of war, this I know
Will the dragons fight for me?
Today we go to fight, in an eternal war
The adventure beginning and already many clans adjoining
Then punctually, at the break of the day, all dragons will attack
Fire, fire, everywhere, killing, killing
Men hacking, blood spilling from hearts and throats
When this war is done, where will I lay down my broken and battered body?
Till the morning of the very next day, for to rise once more
And war will rage once more, this, my new poem, will come your way
Till the end of eternity, there are many tales of dragons to tell
For I am under the spell of many tales!

A Soldier's Funeral
by Eliza Bowditch

A procession down Main Street
Pain, sorrow, anger, fear, all there
But all hidden by one simple question
Why, why must one golden life fade into the distance?
Like the dust of a passing car
Wrapped up in a long line of statistics of roadside bombs and insurgent attacks
"Why did he have to die?" sobs a weeping mother
Clinging to her stern faced husband
The young widow laying white lilies
On the American flag folded over the coffin
Every day, news of death, needless death
And somewhere there are witnesses to a soldier's funeral

Cry
by Brooke Healy

I said my heart is broken into two, you said there is nothing I can do
Every night when I would cry
Wished that I could hold you tight or I felt as if I would die
Now at night when I cry, I just think of crying more and more
And pretending I was in your arms
Once again for being safe, I would laugh at all the memories we shared
That are no more because I don't have you

A Moment Just For Me
by Arturo Partida

Running through the forest I see
A big bird flying free
This part of the world seems out of harm
I feel the breeze pass my arm
It's like a giant happy sea
A moment just for me
I feel like that bird flying free
In this land forever I would like to be
Happiness grows, sadness slows
Sweet smells come through my nose
Through the trees I hear a call
And my spirit begins to fall
It's time to go
But my heart says no

Summary
Summer
by Perrin McCusker

Summer is fun
I swim all day
Almost done
I catch some rays
The cold ice cream
Melts onto the tar
I watch the surf team
From the roof of the car
Long beach night cookouts
Summer food
I am on the lookout
In a sad mood
School's back
New grade
Good to see friends
But miss the summer sun

The Years Just Flew By
by Lauren LaPlant

Passing through the years, kindergarten through six
We had so much fun and we have worked so hard
But it was worth the great experience of school
We will always remember all of our teachers
Who enriched our hearts and minds

Winter Mornings
by Emma Pykosz

The sun is high in the morning sky
It makes me want to jump for joy
When I see children sledding
On the white, gleaming hills
The grass and the flowers cling to life
Under the frozen ground
I can smell woodstoves burning wood
Smoke coming from chimneys
Is against the bright blue sky

Lance Armstrong
by Evan Theroux

Seven times, he won it all, over the hills of France
All along the route, people did cry, "Lance, Lance, Lance"
His wins were sweeter because of his strife
Not just to win a race, but also to save his life
Cancer hit him hard; they said he wouldn't race anymore
He fought for his life as if it was another tour
He sells yellow bracelets to give others a chance
That's why my hero is Lance, Lance, Lance

Grandmother
by Kadeem O'Shane McCarthy

Not my mom, not my brothers, or my dad
Nor any other family member that I've ever had
Compares to the one I'm writing this for
She's not rich, nor is she poor
She makes me cookies when I'm sore
I lived with her when I was four
I love her so much, she's so cool
I wish I could bring her to school
I know you would love her, 'cause she's so nice
And there is no other than my grandmother

Laying In the Yard
by Cody Maggard

Laying in the yard
That's my special place
Clouds drift through the sky
Laying in the soft, green grass
Like heaven sounds of dogs
Splashing in the creek
Cars vroom up the highway
Fried chicken scent soaring of the window
Wind gently blowing my hair
Laying in the yard
That's my special place

Katilyn
by Charla Hamilton

Messy, sloppy, out of control
Tall and broad, brownish blonde hair
Species unknown, dresses okay
A friend of mine nonetheless
Kind and smart, but no better than the rest
Loves to eat, loves to sleep
Loves to play video games, Halo 2 is the best
Has pierced ears, scared of clowns
F18 hornet lover
A good friend no matter what
Dark green eyes, hair's a fluff
Loyal and true
My best friend, through and through

Memories of the Sea
by Jasmine Bragg

I can taste the salt in the air
I can feel the wind in my hair
I can see the waves tearing at the shore
From the window of my hotel door
From the beach I see a fish
Then to myself I make a wish
I wish this day would last forever
And these memories I shall always remember

Dreams
by Jessica Moreira

Do you wonder about dreams, hope, and life?
Do you believe in Heaven or the spirit world?
Does the pain in your dreams awaken you?
Do you wake up in pain, sorrow, and fright?
Do you sleep all through the night?
Do you see faces as you sleep, but for some reason you just can't speak?
Do you feel fingers creeping up your back?
Or is it just a lack of feeling like you can't move at all?
When you wake up do you see shadows in the shapes of your nightmares?
Do you wonder how to get out as if you can't bear to shout?
Do you wonder if your mind is playing tricks or is it just for real?
Are you afraid to turn around for if you do your heart might begin to pound?
Do you wonder if you crossed the line, as if you think you're about to run out of time?
Is what I am saying true; well, that is all up to you?

My Mom's Smile
by Lotoya Jeffrey

I love my mom very much
I know she loves me twice as much
To see my mom smile
Some could walk a mile
Her smile is really special
Like a rare flower blossoming
My mom's smile is rare
Her teeth are clear
Or some might say white
She will smile once in a blue moon
That is a wonderful sight
Don't worry, she'll smile soon

A Day of Freedom
by Matthew Fabiszak

As I sit along the shore
I get ready to explore
And as I set sail on that windy day
I see the other boats zoom throughout the bay
But I and my little ship could make it with a hop and a skip
I take a last look at my map of Tuckernuck
I know I could make it with a bit of luck
But once I put my boat in the water and when she began to totter
And how the other ships looked so big compared to my little rig
I said goodbye to no one when I knew I needed to get away, as far as one could run
And there I sat with the hot sun and set my sails to a run
It was beautiful to get away, I almost cried when I couldn't see the bay
For I left all the stress to find my own place and rest
After hours of the beautiful calm wind and waves free from the dark caves
There was land in sight
I had reached the end of the tunnel that was my bright light
Then I yelled in joy, "Land!", as I dropped anchor on the soft sand
I jumped into the bright blue sea for it was calling me
"Come and play, you must stay"
Splash! I went along with all the stress
I know this was the best
Alone at the beach
And in my mouth lay a delicious peach
I said to myself, "This must be Heaven"
I checked my watch and saw it was seven!
The sun had set
With all those colors looking as though caught in a net
I pulled out my tent
The only place I could afford the rent
Then I lay looking back at my day
When I knew I would have to go back to that dreaded bay
O how I wish I could stay!
It was time to go
And when some would feel low
I was full of joy
For I felt I was a young boy
But when I got to that bay
I couldn't say I felt that gay
But I knew I had been relieved
And now I could believe
It's good to get away
Even if it's just for a day

The Ocean
by Stephen P. Fucaloro and Alex Mandragouras

All is calm and soft as silk
People on the beach are enjoying coconut milk
At any moment, the sea could change
The ocean has forever been strange
The ocean has always been a wonder
Such as, what goes on down under?
But when the night falls
The fierce waves don't stall
The waves sound like bombs, destroying the shores
The maidens of the sailors stare out from their doors
Some men can't be saved
Castaway to a watery grave
The ocean will show no mercy or restraint
In the distance, the glow from the lighthouse looks faint
Finally, the sun peeks its head
Celebrations for the sailors that aren't dead
The night is done, there is no more
Now the light waves kiss the shore

Dedham, Massachusetts
by Scottie Campbell

Dedham is the home of America's first tax supported public school
Established in 1635
Dedham is a suburb of Boston
Has the oldest wooden framed house in America
Also the county seat for Norfolk County
My beautiful hometown

Massachusetts had the first Post Office in America
About 8 out of 10 residents live in cities
Sports teams are the Red Sox, Patriots, Bruins, and Celtics
State nickname is the Bay State
American Elm is the state tree
Capital is Boston
Has many interesting landmarks
Use land for various things
State known for its cranberries
Everyone likes to vacation on Cape Cod
Technically a commonwealth, not a state
Two popular sports began here: volleyball and basketball
Susan B. Anthony was born here

Kaitlyn Dotson

It may come as a shock,
but Kaitlyn is wild about horses.
She loves all animals, but really enjoys riding
and caring for her two horses and two ponies.
Western is her style of choice,
and while just out of the sixth grade, she is a seasoned rider.
Her passion is unmistakable
as embodied in the lines of her award winning poem.

Wild Horses
by Kaitlyn Dotson

The wind whips your mane
Like the ocean tosses a wave
The sweet smell of dew-tipped grass
Tickles your every breath
Hoofs pound the earth
As dirt flies up around you
Holding your long tail up high
A flag signaling behind
The rain thuds against your back
Soaking you to the skin
You dry in the warm, bright, shining sun
That makes your coat glisten
Lassos the cowboys throw
Twirl like snakes around you
Jumping first to the left and then the right
Managing to avoid every one
Racing across the plains
Galloping at top speeds
This is all you have ever known
You are wild, free

Caitlin Fallahay

When Caitlin isn't reading or writing poetry
she may be found playing the obo
in her school's philharmonic orchestra.
She is also a member of the chess club
and enjoys playing soccer and pampering her two cats.
Caitlin tells us the inspiration for her poem, "Missing Them"
is a dream she once had.
This explains the very ethereal quality of her work
which we found to be very powerful.
Congratulations Caitlin.

Missing Them
by Caitlin Fallahay

Girl among the gravestones, lighted by the crescent moon
Near the stroke of midnight
The ghosts draw her here, here to slip away
She stops in front of a sculpted angel, a raised cross
She fingers them gently while a tear races from her eye to her cheek
A trickle of blood tracing down her memory
Lying down, protected by stone wings
Reliving the past, the pain, the tears
Pressing herself against the cold, hardened ground
As if trying to find her mother and sister there, alive and warm again
Girl among the gravestones, despair pouring from her eyes
Straightens to a sitting position
Looks to the stars as if to say, "I'm coming home"
She fades into the darkened sky

Division III

Grades 8-9

Red Sox
by Matthew Cronin

It has been two years since the famed championship gold
And now the team resembles little of that one of old
We have lost a Boston icon and the Idiot and the Caveman
Now it is the Yankees that cheer, "We love you, Damon!"
But now it is time to move on and start a new crusade
Who knows? Maybe there will be a two "K" six parade
Now the rotation is stronger and the team has new found speed
Papelbon's performance is just what any team needs
With Cocoa Crisp's lightning speed, we find he's stealing bases
Curt Schilling and Josh Beckett are the Red Sox's new two aces
Theo's come and Theo's gone, but will always come in
Whenever a big trade is made to help the Red Sox win
So even though the fans have went and gone to buy new jerseys
Of Crisp, A.J., and Willy Mo, and of Josh Beckett surely
We still can see the same old sight of Papi, Manny, Troy
Which makes us thankful of the players that we still have got
So go, play ball, go win the crown, and bring it back to Boston
So what if Johnny Damon's gone, we still think you are awesome

Favorites
by Pauline Situ

Mom and Dad say that they don't have a favorite child
"We love you all the same," they say
But we all know that it's not true, they do have a favorite
Dad would most likely favor his son, since the son would carry on the family name
Mom would favor the one that is most needy, or the one who listens to her
That child in Mom's eyes will always remain her little baby, her perfect little angel
As for those who aren't the favorites, they are usually left alone, cast aside
An outcast to that perfect little family, Mom and Dad leave them alone
Thinking that they will take care of themselves
And devote all their attention to their favorite
When you get hurt, you go tell them
And they'll just tell you to be more careful, be stronger
When you are in so much pain, you cry
And they will tell you to suck it up and be more like your sibling over there
You should suck it up like they say, and look on the bright side
Now there's no one to tell you what you can and can't do
You're free to do whatever you please, but always remember that
Your parents still love you even if they don't show it

They Always Kick You When You're Down
by Samantha Monday

She stands there laughing, as I sit here crying
I try to reach out, but she is gone
Were we ever best friends?
Now, I don't know
We were always so close, now we couldn't be farther apart
We used to be there for each other, now she is only there for herself
She says it's my fault, but what did I do?
She has new friends and has left me alone
She called me the screw up, but look at her now
She has friends, but still has no one at all
She is the screw up, not at all me
She could have had me, but she messed up in her game of life

Unmasked Revelations
by Nida Naushad

A mask slipped on, my duet begins
Strange eyes peer out while I hide within
False smiles greet me, harshly I breathe
I return one warmly but inside I seethe
Two minds, one body; I maintain control
The struggle consumes me, still I remain whole
Alone at last they leave me be
It's in this solitude I'm finally free
The façade falls off, I lack my shield
My reflection burns, the scars revealed

Dream
by Samuel Greenberg

Falling, fighting
Running, never ending
Beyond the realm of reality
Anything can happen
And then you're awake
And it's all over

Friends Forever
by Kathryn Banks

Friendship, no letting down, always there
Running down the halls laughing about inside jokes
Sleepovers, make-up, phone calls
Crying, lots and lots of giggles, tissues
Movie night, The Notebook, using up a whole tissue box
Friendship, no letting down, always there
Love, boys, long instant-messaging conversations
Music, jumping on the beds, singing into hairbrushes
Dance, dancing like no one is watching, standing in front of the mirror
Shopping, trying on everything in the store, not buying a thing
Friendship, no letting down, always there
School, good grades, success, school, bad grades, failure
Parties, invitations for everyone, going overboard
Exaggeration, begging for something, not getting what you want
Friendship, no letting down, always there, hook-ups, break-ups, long phone calls
Laughing, feeling happy, energetic
Candy, craving something unusual, a big mess
Friends forever, always there for you through the good and bad times

Love and Loss
by Amanda Goebel

Red is all around me, I feel that this is real
Red's the only way to express the way I feel
I feel as if my heart will burst from this emotion
All I can draw is hearts, I have no other notion
He gave me a red ruby heart on a chain for my birthday
He told me that he loved me in our own special way
Now I hold his hand so tenderly in mine
And wear my special necklace, my life is so fine
Blue is all I feel now, tears fall from my face
Not one bit of red remains, not a single trace
He is gone away, moved on to someone new
And my red ruby necklace is now the bluest blue
Today I just can't take it, the pain I feel is too great
I begin to write on paper, starting with the date
I write a little letter, then I close my door
I fall onto my bed and cry until I breathe no more

Influence Creates Blurred Vision
by Kelsey Smith

I am tired; do not label me nonsensical
I aspire to become a Hollywood statue
I want to gain your flattery as though I have something worth showing off
But when you put me in an expensive dress and spin me around
It's just suck it in and pass out
I am not suited for such grace (or worth it)
My awkward hands type and erase, write and cross out
I am a criminal in pursuit of what is already mine
But I pretend it isn't, for the sake of saying I've gained something
It's been a while now, and it's loss after loss
Until we're the worst team in the league
(The truth isn't) I feel better starting from the bottom, working my way up
(The truth is) I feel better staying at the bottom and appearing to be on top
Scared of heights, sick of you
I give
Up and down

Who I Am For Who I Am
by Benjamin Tucker

I am from a bike, from Redline and DK
I am from a flower, the tulip's bud
I am from family food, and tattooed biker boys, from Justin, Bobby, Chris and Mike
I am from the pierced holes and the tattoo scars
I am from the guitar whiz Mike
From having to wear a helmet and cleaning my room
I am from the church with long loved friends
I am from Massachusetts, chicken divan and famous scrambled eggs
From the grandparents that love New York, that rubbed onto me
I am from the streets that inherit New York and the Broadway Theater
I am from the country boy brought into the city
I am from the New York love
I am from the cabinet that holds all of our family memories
The wedding band I've taken from my dad
I am from the priceless memories no one can ever take away

Isolation
by Allison Simpson

Behind this door my fate does lie
Often days this door hides the tears I cry
In isolation from the world I must be
Hiding is not so fun, even for a girl like me
On some days it has been my friend
Protecting and hiding me nearly until the end
But some days it just angers me
For I hate being trapped like a cat high up in a tree
Although in hiding is the best place to be
This door doesn't make me feel as safe as I'd rather be
Some days this door makes me feel comforted like my cat
But some days I want to break the door like an old hat
I cannot wait to be free again
Free of this door and ominous land
Although this door has, in a way, become my friend
I wish I could break it down and begin life again

Luna the Moon
by Akiyo Nishimiya

Luna is the Latin name for moon; she shines above our heads
So beautiful and bright, we see her when we crawl into our beds
Each month Luna awakes, fresh and young
As a child she lays in her blue blanket
That is warm, soft and sprinkled with stars
When it rains she is safe and doesn't get wet
Each night she grows bigger and stronger
Half of her face shows through the foggy night
Luna is almost into her adult stage
At that time, Luna will be a creamy white
Luna's adulthood comes and goes
Old age takes over, and she begins to fade
Her light only glows, it doesn't sparkle anymore
The darkness crawls over Luna's crippled body, she is not afraid
The new month comes and with it baby Luna
She shines above our heads, so beautiful and bright
We see her when we crawl into our beds

Dawn of the Dragon's Dynasty
by Ethan Helling

Know as dragon is this creature
Armageddon is the future
Aviating, in the smoke filled air
Feeding off the fear we bear
They've begun our apocalyptic fate
Their purpose is to kill, led only by hate
Survival is difficult and vex
Against the dragons' unforgiving hex
Death comes not by ground, but by air
Leaving annihilation everywhere
Magnificent structures totally abolished
Innocent cities, completely demolished
The ashes of death lie everywhere
While dragons are soaring in the air
Our desolated world of which we now know
Belongs to the beasts, thriving in the fire they blow
This battle of our planet they have won
All we have and cherish is now gone
Where they came from is unknown
We can not return to our ruined home

E Is For Electronic, Not Easy
by Bridget Quinn

The bright screen is staring right back at me
As I beg it for the one thing I need
If it's there, then it's somewhere I can't see
I feel like breaking something as I plead
I wonder why it is taking so long
Maybe something has happened to the thing
And I can't help but think something went wrong
If it finally comes, I know I'll sing
I had sent it over a week ago
I thought that by now I'd have a reply
But I knew that she wouldn't stoop that low
Frustrated, I let out a giant sigh
I know I cannot take this much longer
And so I sit here, silent and somber

Think About the Rest
by Colin Stahl

The burning fire on the shore of night so dark and dreary
The threat of war and largest storm makes people very weary
The winds, they blow, and tides, they turn; the water gleams and glistens
Yet most of this will be ignored for some will never listen
The storm, it grows, and moonlight shows, now people are a bustle
And as storms slow, the families know emergency has rustled
Though damage and destruction is too much to ever bear
Some people help the others just because they truly care
The feelings at a time like this is torture at its best
So some need to stop helping themselves and think about the rest

The Ax of Rock
by Andrew Dougherty

Music is a delicate revolt against the nagging rage the world threw at us
Through our axes of rock
We've weaved a vessel in which we can funnel our wonder, passion, and rage
Through Beethoven's deaf enterprise
He hacked down the oak that stood for the long age, Mozart tore the trend apart
Music's not a mere art, but a gut feeling from the heart
Centuries past, inches went metric, as acoustic went electric
Mozarts of modern age hacked at oaks though extinct
Crowds riled as rhythm and volume interlinked
Forgotten is the exam, our minds are one with Pearl Jam
New oaks were set sprout as we got the Led out
Deep Purple planted twelve chords too revolutionary to write about
We, who've never even held an ax, have the potential to push rock to the max

The Sleep
by Quinn Worthington

The ever-standing words echo in my mind
Those safe faces I've come to love have come to harm me
I fumble and scramble to escape and flee
Try as I might, I cannot break these chains
I yearn for purpose and meaning
Do not break character, do not let them in
Never live nor dead, just being
As the river flows and the pond sits still, as must I
Dependence is death, independence is death
Lost

A Video Game
by Lloyd McKenzie

I'm really not sure why it is so
Why we kids flock to these foolish things
We see them in gifts, boxes, and shelves
We beg and weep to play these things
To devour a game and move to the next
Our crazed addiction is never sated
We're addicts, hooked on things made from bits and bytes
Once we get our hands on one of these games, we play and play
Never stopping nor resting until our parents drag us away in the middle of the night
And we always find time to play these games until we finish one
And our addiction is still strong
We have no use now for a beaten game
And discard this game with the other hundred to move on to the next game
Where the cycle repeats
And the hunger is sated for the time that the game is used
Until the hunger rises again, a hunger that never disappears

Best Friends
by Whitney Wolf

You have been there for me
You were the one that made me see how valuable life can be
You listen to me when I talked
And walked with me when I walked
You've chased away my sadness and wiped away my tears
You've been there for me during my teenage years
I will never forget
When you said, "Don't fret
Over a stupid guy"
Or when we sat looking up at the sky
Crazy and messed up pics
All the way to tear-jerking chick flicks
I just wanted to say
I will love you forever and today
You are my best friend
You lend me your hand when I could not stand
Best friends forever is what we will be
Because you were the one that made me see
How valuable a true friend can be

Erasers
by Grant Hermanson

I know you all have come to use a thing called an eraser
When you make a little error you can get it off your paper
Though when it's gone you'll shriek and shout just like you're filled with fear
For when you try to erase again, you'll make a big black smear
But next time you're mad because you have to write a paper
Just think how hard writing would be if we didn't have erasers

Earth
by Carly Bond

I wait, I watch; time walks by
My face weathers, and from the sky
Snow, rain, wind, and sleet
But I stay still and time walks by
Footsteps echo on my slopes
Life begins and also ends
Trees grow, the sun shines
But I stay still and time walks by
Voices echo in my hills
Tides pull along my shores
I will watch as you pass on
But I will stay as time walks by

Real Vampires
by Rachel McKay

Want to see real vampires, I'll tell you where they are
They're your next door neighbors; they're the stranger from afar
But they don't suck blood, or deal with immortality
They're the everybody of today, only less like you and me
They're the rude couple down the street, the murderer downstairs
Even the convenience store clerk, but nobody cares
They're your horrible teachers, the student you despise
It's the prisoner in your head; you can hear the tortured cries
But one day, that vampire will come and wipe away your face
The life you've begun and crafted will be another life gone to waste
You will become one of them, the faceless, dreary crowd
Your days will be humorless, your heart chilled and blackened by a sooty cloud
And all the while you'll be wondering of what you did wrong
But it's too late, you cannot go back, your true self is gone

My Life
by Jeannie Do

Just a couple of minutes before sunrise
I wake up and get ready for school
Wishing that I was still in bed
And wishing that the troubles that are to come will never come
I do my hair the nicest way I can, and pick out the best outfit
Sitting on the train, I wonder how each and every one of them live their life
Is it like mine?
I sit in every single class, checking the clock every five minutes
When it actually hits 2:15
I run out of class and can't wait to have fun with people I care about
I find out that they are going to their friend's house
And they promise that they'll hang out with me tomorrow
This wasn't the first time this has happened
Sitting on the train, I wonder how each and every one of them live their life
Is it like mine?
No, nobody can have a life like mine

The Angel In My Eye
by Jamie Delaney

Sitting, watching
Staring out into the world from a window as the cars go by
Eyes twinkling, shining with the brightest of blue
Foreshadowing the beauty of the heavens
Once homeless, lost, helpless, unknown to love
Not knowing he will be the most loved being ever to reside on Earth
The time has come
We only have one life to live, this lucky one had nine
Never used them sparingly; as the clock ticked, another was gone
All good things come to an end at some point, but why so soon?
Beautiful day, not a cloud in the sky
A perfect passageway and a perfect view for an angel
And so it was meant to be
And then like that, he's gone
Not a chance for a last hug, not a chance to say a last goodbye
Goodbye, goodbye Frisky, the little angel in my eye

To Each Their Own
by Patxi Colbern

With so many religions to pick from
How can we choose the most suitable one?
One's own values amount to a great sum
We can either accept or we can shun
Catholicism is very devout
Yet the Mormons are very united
The Baptists really make me want to shout
Judaism is holy and lighted
All religions have two same basic rules
Be kind and respect a higher power
Anyone can be saved, even the fools
Do all end the same in our final hour?
Hopefully to all, Heaven will be shown
When it comes down to it, to each their own

Tears of the Holocaust
by Amanda Freehoff

I began my life unaware and innocent
In a matter of seconds my life drastically changed in ways that I didn't understand
As I began to understand my fate, horrid thoughts raced through my mind
The evil came in like a tidal wave, crashing down and taking lives
As I came upon my last precious moments, my heart began to beat faster
Tears, tears flow down like raindrops as I finally notice
That this is a fight that I will not win
All hope is lost, except my pride, as I die in the arms of David

Waves Flowing To Rhythm
by Shelby Holden

A distant melody floats; soft, slow, simple
Though something is wrong, there's anger in its being
A stronger verse takes over the melody, my own voice
A beat on top of a small stream, taking control of the waves
The stream expands, taking a new form
An ocean, waves larger than before
I lose control over my voice; the distant melody is now strong
Forcing my voice to fade; soft, slow, nothing
My ship sinks and water replaces, leaving me to drown
Memories of my own voice, gone

Nonsense
by Carlton Hue

Two ducks are waddling in the snow
And their food fell in the cafeteria by the gusty kids
There were many cars driving by the school
And one had killed a deer
I checked my watch to see the time, it was an hour behind
My mom and dad went to see flowers growing on the sidewalk
On my way to school on Essex Road, by the playground I saw a creepy house
Next to the creepy house lies a gym
Many kids were hopping, hopping over obstacles
My friend Ryan assisted his brother and sister to cross the longest bridge
On their way, they saw that boys were riding bikes very fast
From my house, I could hear the yelling of Mr. Sortevik
Out of my window of my car, kids were rapping while walking to school
Spiderwebs in the morning dew
I noticed a pattern on the hallway floor
Calendar says, "Two weeks till vacation!"
The time had changed
One colored car was moving

Jolly Rancher Apple Twists
by Jiayuan Wang

Jolly Rancher Apple Twists come in packages of many
When you hold one up, it is wrapped with a plastic labeled "Jolly Rancher"
Once you feel the smooth plastic wrapper in your hands
You will have an urge to twist both ends and reveal the grand treasure inside
Jolly Rancher Apple Twists, with their distinctive green emerald blend
Are the favorites of children, out of their kind
Their structure and flavor dazzles children
They just cannot resist opening the wrappers
Inside those wrappers contain the Jolly Ranchers themselves
The apple-flavored Jolly Ranchers, in their glorious, golden presence
Are rectangle-shaped, hard rocks
The undying sensation in these rocks ought to leave you thunderstruck
Once you put the rock into your mouth, it will first taste a little like sour apples
But, afterwards, it will be as sweet as fresh, golden honey
The flavor will be everlasting, and it will astonish you

A Cool Little Bro
by Stefanie Ormeche

I love the kid who is my bro
We sing and dance wherever we go
We listen to music and sing them our way
And when we get each other going
Our day just keeps on rolling
We kiss each cheek good night
And during the day, we fight
But when we fight, we know
That we love each other so
So here's something for my little bro
Cool in a way that I love him so

The English Language
by Zachaery Ratzlaff

Hip or not?
Fad or fading?
Was it just "snap" or "snap, crackle, pop"?
Was it fop or just fab!
The English language is a wonderful thing
Full of words and phrases
Of spectacular fun!

Darkness Falls
by Frankie Pagliaro

Darkness falls around the house
The peeper frogs chirp
Darkness falls around the house
The cat lays down for a long nap
Darkness falls around the house
Stars emerge in the black sea above
Darkness falls around the house
The moon opens wide its eyes and begins to ascend
Darkness falls around the house
The air takes on a certain chill
Darkness falls around the house
The world is peaceful
Darkness falls around the house
The night is quiet
Darkness falls around the house

Summer Days
by Amanda Francis

Every day I sit outside in the sun
And watch the flowers sway as the wind blows
Whenever I'm outdoors it's always fun
The grass scent fills the air as someone mows
But this also happens during the night
Because up here the sun doesn't go down
The sun floods the land with all of its light
And when it is rainy we go to town
The days go by and quickly drift away
I hate the thought of my summer ending
It seems like it was just the start of May
In fall school is where I'll be attending
And a new year will start again with books
And few faces with all the summer looks

Lightning
by Ethan Thomas

Bolts crash to the ground
Lighting the dark night sky with
The sound of thunder

Crescendo
by Lindsey Rogers

The lights dim down; the curtains open, silence takes over the room
As the music begins, a dancer appears like a bud that's preparing to bloom
Emotions unsaid, she feels in the music through all the years of her life
Through the pain and tears, through smiles and laughter
Ballet expressed all her joy, love, and strife
Her pain the crowd feels, love and joy they feel too
They are transferred to her world
Her tears are on their face, her joy's in their soul
Her emotions at them are hurled, she sprints then she leaps
Flames burn in her soul, the fire within bursts out!
She's up in the air! She's up on her toes! She's now unstoppable without a doubt
The music slows down, she begins to waltz
But smoldering logs still remain of the flames she had shown
And fires of her soul which now hides deep down, but are there all the same

The Badlands
by Josey Erickson

"He was a short man," whisper the junipers
"He had a mustache," says the blue grass
"This man was a skilled hunter," the animals recall
The snow says, "Trapping was something he enjoyed"
The pinecones say, "He went walking along the creek"
Who was this man?
The kettle says, "I was always put over the fire"
The woodstove remembers, "The house was always warm"
"His favorite was cornmeal," the cooking pot shows
The teakettle says, "There was a woman in the house"
The woodpile says, "Long hours were taken to make me"
Who was this man?
"Skirts swept across me at supper," the floor says
The chimney recalls, "He shot turkey for dinner"
"Long nights were spent by the fire," said the rocking chair
The wagon said, "There were no fields to tend"
The picture of Alice says, "He was loved and cared for"
The great things this man will accomplish

The Sound of Sweet Revenge
by Amanda Lavalley

He has hurt me mentally
Missing my recital just to hang out with friends
Promising to do things and never following through
It's a bunch of little things but eventually, it builds up inside
My anger level rises like the heat of a blazing fire
I am at the highest temperature point
The point where, whenever I think of him, emotionally I blow up
He is getting married now, to someone I don't like
She is having a child
Hopefully, it is not like her other children: bratty and wild
I tell him I no longer want to live with him
He just cries, and cries, and cries
Now I just sit in my room and laugh
Oh, what a wonderful sound
The sound of sweet revenge!

Victim
by Nicholas Parker

"Detective Miller?" The sergeant walks in, "This one is ... interesting"
Interesting, in my job that word can mean any number of things
I walk down to the parking lot in the cold; it is the kind of cold
That shakes you up and slaps you with its frosty fist, Christmas in New York
I see the flashing lights and blaring sirens, cops, I think, and go there
I step into the circle of cars; the victim stains the snow with blood
It looks like a raspberry slushy from hell; I hate this job sometimes
Danny comes up next to me in a trench coat and starts his normal spiel
"The victim was 23, 5'9", Hispanic, no ID on him, shot seven times in the face"
Danny finishes. Yeah, I could see that
I bend over this victim, an innocent man, most likely
Danny starts again, "The trouble is identification. No one knows him"
No one knows him, those words stay with me
This man is dead, and yet no one knows but the force, and me
Perhaps no one even cares about his death
This man has seven holes in his face
And yet he doesn't make a scratch, even a dent
In the minds of the people of New York, who is he?
He is but a lost man, a soul swept up in the ravaging tide of this city
I say, "Get him cleaned up and keep him in the morgue tonight"
Danny's reply, "And after tonight?"
Mine, "Wait for a missing persons report, we'll know him them"
I walk off, if he can't make the dent, I will

Sounds In Anne Frank's World
by Mike Nugent

I hear playing, I hear planes
I hear people suffering great pains
There are children playing, there are Nazis marching
People are hiding, Jews are dying
I can hear it all
It makes me cry
I'm going to die
I hear bangs
The door falls down
I can hear it all, it makes me frown
My time is up, and I must go
The concentration camp is my new home

Calloused Soft
by Tara Daniels

A diminutive diamond is on her hand
Her palms calloused
From the strenuous work she had endured
Although they are coarse
When her daughter sits with her
The rough skin becomes soft once more

A United America
by Olivia Grant

America is known as the melting pot
Our ancestors came here whether they wanted to or not
Pilgrimage, slavery, genocide, communism, treason
Well, whatever the reason
We all must get along; unity is key
If we are to free
Ourselves from bad things that still exist today
Well, that's what I believe and it's what I'll say
America can be oh so crazy
But it doesn't have to be oh so shady
It fact, it can be quite nice
Like clouds which can be as white as rice
If we stick together
And learn how to live with different cultures forever
We can be a great example
For everyone, for every country all over the world

Untitled
by Nicolette MacEachern

Crying mother
Dying girls
Dreaming of another world
Blood filled bathtubs
What I dread
As blind desires
Run through my head
Night falls
And dreams dissolve
As you spin into oblivion

Dawn To Dusk
by Lauren Allegrezza

Fog clearing, my breakfast comes with the morning sun
Pulling my handler along the path
Quickly, quickly, don't dawdle!
For effect, I add in an enthusiastic buck
I spy the dewy grass and bless my luck
Ears pinned, stay away! Stay away!
I must admit I do not like the big bay
Who lives just over the pasture fence
He steals all the emerald green gifts of the ground
So that for me, there are none to be found
Cozy warmth, as evening rises my stomach is fed
And then, of course, I am put to bed
A blanket draped over my glossy haunches
Indeed, it is time for a lovely nap
Though my senses are alert for a possible trap
Sweet scents, a pile of hay is dropped in my stall
The barn lights are dimmed once and for all
Time for me to rest my head
The soft breeze sends me to sleep
And I do not fear the things that creep

Leaving
by Bill Jacoby

She was great, the top of my world
But she is leaving now, she is going away
There is no way to make her stay; I do what I can to keep her here
But she is leaving now, she is going away
I want her back; I can't believe she's going
But she is leaving now, she is going away
She's fading away, a dot on the horizon
I don't feel the irony until the pain hits me
She is gone now, and I know it
She is not coming back, and I know it
I want to cry but not to show it
But anger prevails, and I lose control and show it
I pick up something and throw it
I feel sad, lonely, and lost
How did she leave?
I thought she was perfect
She has now left, she is gone away

Peter Wentz
by Lydia Hogan

With a scribble of his pen, he gives an anthem to the hopeless
He pours his heart onto the paper, for it is his only weakness
He delivers the words through my speakers and the pages of a book
I can sense his heart of darkness with every single stolen look
He's the song I can't stop singing, he's the pill that helps me heal
He's the vampire in the movies, who I know is completely real
Every step he takes I'll follow, though he's going nowhere fast
His lyrics stain my mind like poison, his tattered photos always last
He's the air that keeps me breathing; he's the words that I can't say
He's the monster in my closet, who I love in every way

Serenading the Moon
by Ben Záa Gallagher

I swoon the moon
And play a tune with my sister, June
She played a lute while I, the flute
We played all night
Basking in its soothing light

Misery
by Karen Taborda

I have never felt this way
I don't know the reason why things happened this way
My house, it is destroyed
My parents are divorced, and my best friend betrayed me
It was my entire fault for always trusting my best friend
And for thinking that my parents were always going to be together
I have always been part of the problem and never the solution
I don't know what to do with my life, everything seems so difficult
I am alone in this world
Being in this world is like being in Hell
People try to pretend they are happy
But in reality, they are even more miserable than me
I never received any love from my parents
Sometimes they just pretended that I wasn't there
They never loved me, and they never will

Pillows
by Rachel Filkins

White puffy pillows
Fluffy clouds from the nighttime sky
Soft ground that covers heaven
Pfff
Smooth, silky sheets
Whiter than snow
Cottony bunches of marshmallows
Sleeping year-round
Swwsh
Cool, cushiony cushions
Lounging about all day

Basketball
by George Bekandy

I like to shoot the ball at an angled arch
I bring down the hoop, and they watch my feet dangle
Once in a while, I pass an alley-oop
I like slam dunks that take me to the hoop
I wish to watch every single game
The Celtics are a team to name
Pierce is one of their greatest players
A great team leader and a defensive ozone layer
Another team to name is the Miami Heat
That is a team that cannot be beat
Shaquille O'Neal is like no other
He treats his teammates like his younger brothers
But I have to admit, the greatest player is M.J.
Try to recall when he scored 63 points in one day
That was when everyone wanted to play M.J.'s way
And when he took the game winning fade away
Yes, basketball is my favorite sport
I love to dribble on the court
What can I do, this game is so addicting
My love for this game cannot be abolished

Who Are We?
by Monique Dallal

You look at me with closed eyes
With not a clue of who I am
Why I am here sitting beside you
Here today, in the pouring rain
Second by second, new ideas rush through my mind
Trying to comprehend what you are thinking
Wondering if you know who I am
Now, what I am wondering, how did you change like this?
One year relaxing by the pool side
Now sitting confused in a home
Everyone around you looks so old
You, the ones around you, look as if they do not have a care in the world
The room is filled with a depressing mood
Why did you have to get Alzheimer's?
Why, how could you change so much in only one year?

In Pursuit of Five Hundred Dollars
by Anna Frappaolo

It's really not that critical
But I must confess
I tend to be competitive
I have to do my best
To write a poem, don't fret it
But then again, I could win a prize
Oh, what to write about
To catch the judges' eyes?
I could write about my best friend
No, that would be too sappy
Perhaps I'll write something serious
Or something light and happy
I could mimic poets like Joyce Kilmer
You know, the guy who wrote "Trees"
But I find that stuff so boring
It brings me to my knees
Alas, I still don't have a subject
And it's the end of the day
I guess I'll just hand this in
I hope I'll win, anyway

Racing Against the Wind
by Helen Lee

Hairs are flying in front of my eyes
As I soar through the streets and let my soul fly
I feel the heat rising and rushing to my head
As I race through the streets and let my thoughts flutter
I smell the fresh spring air as I jog through the park
And taste the bitter saltiness of the sweat running down my own forehead
I stop a while to take a breath, but only for a while
So I can start up yet again with my relaxing morning jog
Nice, easy, and relaxed, I race home to yet another beautiful day
Chasing all my troubles away as I race against the morning wind

Serenity
by Matt Sivazlian

A mocking bird stares at the placid surface of a shallow pond
It stares as a single drop of dew slowly falls into the untouched sea of glass
Ripples spread outward, disrupting the calm
A cool fog makes its way to the water
Enveloping the trees in an eerie mist
The bird now spreads its wings
A series of songs erupts from its throat as it soars above the trees
The cool air, refreshing breeze in its face as it flies

Plastic Heart
by Ada Lin

There once was a girl named Sally
Who played hopscotch on the street
But one day, Sally slipped and fell
And her heart broke on concrete
So Sally went to the corner store
Where they sold hearts for a cent or two
Sally bought a plastic heart
All shiny, nice, and new
Now Sally walked right down the street
Her blue eyes empty and cold
For as shiny as Sally's new heart was
A plastic heart can't feel

Momma, I Am Slipping
by Ngoc Doan

Momma, I am slipping
Slipping from your warm vibration
The world I could not help but knowing
The truth you saved me from realization
A worried-free childhood you gave me
Only a memory as I recall
Love was the only thing that I receive
Where knees scraped and innocent bawl
Momma, I am slipping
A world I am yet to see
Tears have been rolling
Only now I can perceive
Another side of life keeps on unraveling
Momma, I do not want to believe
The nightmare that is reviving
Will I be able to accept what I receive?

Outside
by Hadi Haidar

When you walk outside it feels so good
If I could stay there every second, I really would
The sky is blue and beautiful to look at
Unless it is covered by clouds that are big or flat
The grass can be amazing, if it is healthy and green
And the air can be soothing, if it is unpolluted and clean
Trees are plentiful, green, and tall
But they can also be colorful, empty, or small
Houses can be big, long, or new
And they can be small or old all the way through
The people outside can be nice or mean
And there is more in the world than you have ever seen
You see many common animals, like a cat or dog
But rarely see something like a groundhog
You can play sports with friends just for fun
Or you can play a game that involves you to run
Life is great, especially when you are outside
If I can't be there, I'd rather just hide

The Dream
by Lauren Rasmussen

In his dream he saw a beautiful girl
She looked like an angel sent from Heaven
Her smile was wide, each tooth was like pearl
Her voice was calm as she said, "Hello, Kevin"
Kevin then smiled as he gave her a rose
He spoke of his love while on bended knee
He said, "I love your long hair and your nose"
She then said, "Kevin, you make me happy"
Kevin danced with merriment and excitement
The girl, named Marie, danced along with him
He proposed, and on a honeymoon they went
They ended up with a daughter named Kim
But suddenly, when they were arm in arm
Off went Kevin's loud, obnoxious alarm

Walking the Beach
by Johnna Lynch

Walking along the crowded beach
The shimmering ocean just within my reach
The soft sand in between my toes
And the hot sun glazing upon my nose
Loud waves crashing on the shore
Sounding like a lion's roar
People swimming and yelling too
Acting like they're monkeys in a zoo
I found sea shells in the sand
I had to hold them tightly in my hand
The chirping seagulls swooping down
Then I saw someone give a frown
The seagulls had taken their lunch
They thought they might have a munch
It is about time to go home
I have to call my friend on the phone
I will tell her about my walk
Maybe she'll come next time so we can talk

A Girl
by Jenny Hoac

There's a girl, she's X years old and lives at place
This bird trapped in a cage, no one can get in and she cannot get out
They don't see the cage, not the bird within
All they see is the mask over the face, over the attitude of a devil
And so, the bird sings, and so she sings, singing within, sweet songs of sorrow
Crying in her little cage, no one to help, no one to know
She doesn't know why she's trapped; she can't see the face of this devil
She cannot tell who it is; she's confused, lost, alone
This is a girl X years old living at place, she's named so and so, and she's trapped
She's a candy coated, pitch black rock
You see a semi-harsh, semi-sweet, all around lost girl
A girl lost in her own depressed little world
And no one, nowhere, with nothing, can ever set her free and save her

Greek
by Nick Desjarais

There once was a man who knew a Greek
His family lived on a creek
His sister fell in
And grew a fin
And the family had rushed to the geek

KC
by Katlund Iandosca

Kitten so cute and sweet
It's funny when she licks my feet
The way she stares, the way she plays
She always lightens up my days
So comfortable she is on my bed
Sprawled out and resting her head
What she's thinking, nobody knows
Her nose as pink as a rose
Thank goodness it was her I chose
Her tummy fur as white as snow
I just can't ever let her go
She is my baby
She is KC

Family
by Vincent Coronity

Families are special because no matter what you do they stick with you
You can change many things
But you can never change your family which may be bonded by rings
Blood or even adoption, abandoning family is never an option
A family loves you and protects you, too
But even if they say
That our family does not let anyone get away with anything, they do!
This is true!
Younger brothers, sisters, and even cousins
Our parents, aunts, and uncles protect them but not us in the dozens
Families do care and share feelings with one another
But if a little, "Boo-hoo" from the young ones, and oh brother!
They whine, cry, and bother you when you're having a good time
But you can never say goodbye, oh why?

Our Eyes Meet
by Elodie Paquette

I see you walking in that way that you do
With your jaunty stride, releasing an aroma of confidence, so unlike me
Yet I convince myself, that we are the same, perfect for one another
As you walk by me our shoulders touch, our eyes meet, and you smile
For a second, just one second, I actually believe that I mean something to you
But I wonder, among all the others you see, am I just another face in the crowd?

Shadows of Hell
by Christopher Talbot

Behind the shadows of the gates of Hell
I walk my dark path of death and evil
Many have come, many have gone
My life's purpose is to show them the burning gates of death
I was born as the damned, though I did not choose this fate
I walk beside the silent stream, the silent stream of blood from all the dead
This place is only the beginning for me and all I have damned
For when I open the gates, those gates that lead to my dark demise
The raging inferno of Hell will rise and burn the Earth to a black cinder
My path of darkness and death, behind the shadows of my father
Will continue, until every place of light is covered in darkness
And my silent stream of blood flows through all eternity

Ray
by Alex Gifford

Move his fingers across the bright board
Not knowing by sight, but by sound
Taps his foot on the pedals to keep the color alive
Can never see the joyful smiles of the crowd
Never can see the happy faces
Never the smiles of a shark
Yet see them in his mind's eye
Laughs a great big laugh
Then thinks about where the white keys are
On that shiny black and white board
And plays to his heart's delight

Carousel
by Rich Liang

Spin blue, the horses run, stop, red
Brightly glow the seats of gold
Gather as princes and princesses on a journey
Goes heroically and like a fairy tale dream
Spin, spin, spin, stop
A happy ending, a dragon slain
Stay for the wedding, no?
Vivid the sparks of thoughts
Imagination runs wild like wild things
A kaleidoscope of flashing rainbows
Let me spin and spin my own world

Love
by Andrea McElroy

Love is unique; love is so sweet
Love sweeps you off of your gentle, small feet
Love is a feeling that you have inside
No one will take it from you; no matter how hard they try
Love is no battle, just a warm feeling
Love is unique, and careful, and giving
Love is not touch or feelings on skin
Love is a feeling, a feeling that you're in
Your brain has a small heart that is hidden inside
Think more than touch or you will be smacked in surprise!

Anne Frank Remembrance
by Amanda Paulauskas

We will remember
The joy she brought throughout the Annex
She danced and sang when everybody was gone
She felt as if she was always being hated for being herself
She was joyful through the good and the bad
Even when she thought she was mad
Whenever things went really bad, she would never cry
But she did get scared as time passed by
The green police were oh, so frightening
The Nazis were the worst, they terrified her at times
Eventually, they would be the cause of her death
As time passed by she wondered, "Why me?"
As her diary closed for the last time
Her words faded away, her voice became faint
Anne slipped away into the Nazis' grasp
At the camp, she would breathe her very last breath

Friends and Family
by Olivia Collins

Where do you look when you're in trouble?
Who do you need when you're stuck in a bubble?
A shoulder to lean on when you need to cry
An ear that listens and a mouth that sighs
The people you need are always there
Giving advice that you want to hear
Best friends are the ones who laugh and complain
The ones who care and make you insane
Family helps too when something goes wrong
And on holidays, you party and talk for so long
They help during times, the good and the bad
Whether or not you're happy or sad
Cousins are there to laugh and to play
Parents are there just so they can pay
Sisters help to discuss you and your life
Brothers are there to say something nice
Aunts help to clean bruises and cuts
Uncles tell jokes and make you go nuts
Family and friends are needed to survive
They're the ones that we live with all of our lives

Anne Frank, We Remember
by Matthew Allen

You will never be forgotten, your smile true and bright
You endured those times of struggle, always trying to be right
There was once a time of pleasure, innocent, and unafraid
Oh, those blissful days back then, many games with friends you played
Amid the joy and laughter, a storm advanced with lightning force
A hurricane of hatred, composed of men without remorse
Slowly throughout Europe, an evil epidemic began to crawl
It choked the roots of diversity; for help of Christians, Jews did call
You ran away from home, before the Nazis did arrive
You were in a secret place, where your family might survive
Many ruthless men patrolled, killing those who dared disobey
They set up concentration camps, murdering hundreds everyday
Two years your family hid, "End this war," you prayed
Then a sudden glimpse of light, the allies did invade!
Inches from your freedom, so close to liberation
The Nazis found you out, would there be any salvation?
Your family split into pieces, some over here and over there
Without a chance of living, it was hard not to despair
You will never be forgotten; it's you we ought to thank
We learned to seek the good in people from you, a hero, Anne Frank

Lost At Sea
by Meghan Lowney

He is lost, adrift at sea
Tumbling about in unfamiliar waters
Searching madly for shore
The water grows rougher, and he continues on
Knowing that this is a phase that will be over soon
Relentlessly, he is pounded, but he doesn't give up
It's not in his nature
Tired and weary, he drops
Beginning to ask himself
"What have I done to deserve this fate? Why me? Why now?"
He cries and waits
Hoping and praying that it will all end soon
But prayers do not stop storms
And hopes alone cannot keep men alive

Sincerely, Your Friend
by Emily Donner

I can't believe that just last night, I'd gone to that party
At first it was some innocent fun, but it began to get rowdy
It wasn't my intention, peer pressure made the call
But now I'm lying on the floor, because of alcohol
At first I only had a sip, but then I had some more
Now with colors all distorted, I'm here on the floor
Noises filling up my head, it's difficult to speak
I couldn't make it up the stairs; I'm feeling much too weak
I'm sorry that I did this, Mom and Dad and sisters
After all that vomiting, my throat is filled with blisters
You know I'll always love you, but I have to pay the price
For drinking at that party, now I know it wasn't right
I feel my heart is slowing; I can't even lift my head
The pain is near unbearable, I wish that I were dead
The lights are dull and fuzzy, and I can hardly hear
Oh, how much better I would feel if I knew you were near
My fingers feel so icy cold, my stomach burnt away
I wish I could see you once more, to live another day
Tell them all I'll miss them, that I'll love them to the end
But I can hear God calling now, sincerely, your friend

The Horse Who Touched My Heart
by Tess Wilkinson

The sound of his hooves fall hard on the ground
The warmth of his breath lands sweet on my neck
A gelding he was, my favorite mount
Antsy he was, he'd stand only for a sec
A beautiful coat and a nose so soft
The years I spent with him, mine till the end
Riding on his back sent my mind far off
Day by day we grew closer, my best friend
A great listener, we shared everything
Whenever I left, my heart grew sore
He knew how to care, not saying a word
We always had fun, no day was a bore
He may be leaving, no matter how far
I'll always love him, my sweet Taladar

Noises of the City Night
by Sylvia Chang

I laid there, my eyes half closed
In a dark room with silence
Then, all of a sudden, something awakes me
The noises that make me incense
Motorcycles raced by
Disrupting the silence that exists
Then the ambulance hastens past
With the siren that persists
I hear the booming music
From the car it rumbles
I hear the constant quarrel
But no detail of the grumbles
The different sounds that keep me aroused causes me to recite
"How could I fall asleep, with all the noises of the city night?"

Two Words
by Hanna Wolsfelt

Hate, love
Both words with four letters, one used for worse, one used for better
They're thrown around a lot, like spices being thrown into a big soup pot
Two friends try on a dress, only one it fits
"I hate you," says the one it doesn't, but does she really mean it?
A couple has gone out for a month and they haven't split
"I love you," says the boyfriend, but does he really mean it?
I myself have not felt either of these things
Hopefully I will never hate, but with love my heart will sing

The Trail of Life
by Savannah Clemens

We've traveled this trail
Along the rail
Of the rocky road called life
There's been our share of sorrows, happy and bright times, too
And glorious times when we've let the light of grace shine through
But now, it's come to an end
I've walked through all the bends
Can't wait to do it again
In some other life somewhere, outside time

Singing
by Elle Brigida

My mouth is the door to my soul
It opens
Out comes my heart bouncing along the notes
My soul sneaks out gliding along the staff
My mouth shuts
Ending my moments of pure vulnerability
I await the moment when my heart will once again collide with the melody
My heart is forever beating
To the rhythm of the music that pulses through my veins
The harmony bubbles inside of me
Overflowing once the pathway to my being opens once again

Loraine
by Jennifer O'Malley

There once was a dame by the name of Loraine
No one liked poor Loraine for she was quite gross and a tad insane
She growled like the Hulk but carried more bulk
Her teeth were so large; she could bite through a barge
Her hair was a mess, a sack was her dress
Her stench was so vile it cleared out the Nile
She waved her arms and stomped her feet, not a very pleasant person to meet
So all people stayed clear when Loraine was near

The Beach
by Kaitlyn Butler

The beach, soft sand squishing between toes
Glistening water reflecting the setting sun
As a cool sea mist wisps across your face
Noisy seagulls squat around lazily
And the scent of fresh salt fills the air
The beach, searching for colorful seashells
Shovels and pails in hand
Climbing the jetty as water splashes against the rough surface
And searching for tiny crabs scrambling within the crevices of the rocks
The beach, night falls as the glare from the lighthouse becomes visible
Hearing the grass weeds among the sand dunes whistle in the breeze
The crackling of a warm fire and sound of waves crashing in the background
How I wish I were at no other place than the calm, relaxing setting of the beach

Confusion Through Destruction
by Glennon Montgomery

We are all confused about why people are abused
When people step on planes and burn in deadly flames
But that answer is so simple when you live in the USA
With the President causing chaos and dismay
People's minds are not so blind when 9-11 comes to mind
We think of the search that is on today
That started with a tragedy that seems like yesterday
It started in New York, moved on to Washington, DC
Ended in Pennsylvania, flight number 93
I was only in class when two planes broke the glass
The glass of two buildings standing tall
These buildings went down with a heavy fall
September 11 is the date
When brilliant people met their fate

This Is Me (Remix)
by Marlin Mendoza

Who am I? Man, I don't even know, all I know is that I'm a poet
I can't be scared, I gotta show it
I might not win contests with my poems, that's ok
I'm getting stronger with my lyrics, you will be blown away
So don't be looking at me, because I'll leave you with nothing to say
You can holla at me because I live in EC, can you dig that?
You can't see me; c'mon, I'm on my way to fame
You looking at me like my rhymes are lame, let's go!
You know you like my lyrics, it's a nice flow, this is who I am
I can't try to be someone else because I am what I am

Your Words
by Charlotte Hough

Your words are daggers, etching graffiti into the walls of my soul
Unwanted writings, yet inevitably written
They cannot be erased, only scratched out; covered up but never will they be gone
Your eyes burn through my skin, peeling it away bit by bit
Until all that is left is my heart, open and vulnerable, defenseless to your actions
One squeeze and it shatters into pieces, never to be whole again
Your expression is cold and empty; you keep your emotions well hidden
One board pried open from your closet door, and all that is revealed is empty space
Not a trace of spirit; only your murderous words

Love Story
by Ann Situ

I stay up all night thinking about our fight
I reach for the phone because I feel all alone
I'm missing my baby, but I'm still angry
He should be saying sorry, he left me at that party
He tells all these lies, my suspicions arise
He tells me he loves me, saying this too easily
As I reached for the phone, it's as if I had already known
I had heard no ringing, but now my heart's singing
Because my baby's saying sorry, and that he loves me
All those lies mean nothing anymore, and knowing this makes me soar

Dream
by Tabatha Hudson

A guy so tender and sweet
So gentle to me and like a dream
His dark hair like black, reminds me of the night sky
So gentle and caring; he would always be there just for me
Once a best friend, now a boyfriend
Like we were meant to be forever together
He is just a dream with black hair and brown eyes
And a voice that makes the heavens sing
Soft skin like rose petals, but he is only a dream

The Call
by Ruth Tejada

When my heart soars to Heaven
With my grandfather holding hands
Laughing and flying in the sunset
Dreaming about a better world with no suffering
Not hearing the agonizing cries of children
Instead, I hear joyful laughter
And I rejoice at the thought of a brand new day
That's when I think of happiness
And the elaborate colors of spring
And the smell of ripe coconuts
Daydreaming ... a step away from reality
But when I wake up, my thoughts are arranged
And this is when I take action

Little Friend
by Max Batchelder

My little silver friend sits on the floor
Always sitting, ever immobile
He sits, humming his favorite tune
Like a silver box full of bees
His hum is continuous
Like a ticking clock, or a memory
Just something we all identify
But never fully notice
Until it stops when the world grows dark
He hums louder when thinking
About math and writing
But mostly he just hums to himself
He can talk without speaking
But only to his quieter, newer friends
He can draw as Michelangelo
Yet has never held a pencil
He's the newest addition to the family
My little tomato
My little silver one
My computer

First Place
by Corrine Hillman

Ready, set, bang!
The gun goes off
Millions of pounding feet booming against the rock solid Earth as fast as lightning
A pack of frightened gazelles gracefully leaping away from the enemy
Steamy, hot faces swiftly stride toward their destination
Hearts wildly beating against the pattern of rushing feet
Faster, faster, boom, boom
Like thunder in a rapid storm
As land is seen by sailors who have traveled for months
The finish line peeks up around a sharp corner as if playing hide-and-seek
Faster, faster, boom, boom
Feet pounding, hearts beating against expanded chests
Lungs gasping for air, bodies struggling to stride any farther
Stop! The destination is found, the finish line behind
First place

Football
by Brian Sitcawich

The air is filled with the sounds of people yelling, the pressure is almost unbearable
The plan is decided, everyone must work together in order for it to work
The men line up and prepare themselves
All of their hard work has led up to this moment
The play begins
The exhausted players use their last bit of energy for this final try
The clock runs out, this is it
This is football
The quarterback drops back to pass, the ball is thrown down the field
An eerie silence falls on the stands; every head is turned toward the end zone
The ball soars into the hands of the receiver, touchdown!
This is football

This Powerful Green
by Matt Elkin

It's funny how the color green can mean so many things
It can be good or bad, or anywhere in between
Green like the leaves on the trees that give us oxygen
Or green like the color of money for wars; makes me say, "Not again!"
On one side, it's the color that keeps us alive
And on the other, it's the color that ends thousands of lives
In the fall, this green turns into different colors
The same shade of those fighting, fallen sisters and brothers
The difference is, people enjoy seeing the yellow and red
But don't enjoy watching the news, hearing about those who are dead
And have died fighting for this cause
And our country's laws and it makes me pause
And I think, is this what money has done?
Has left wives crying, holding their baby sons
Because they've lost a husband, a dad, and a friend
And in their heart they know that this madness will never end
So when people see green they get different emotions
See the leaves and those overseas, sailing the ocean
But what happens when these leaves begin to fall?
I think life would be better with no green at all

Sharing Secrets
by Megan Scipione

Keeping secrets can do many things, they can console, comfort, protect
But sometimes, just sometimes, sharing those secrets can help people connect
When you have a secret you seem cut off
You change your ways, everyone else is brushed off
You need to tell someone, what's stopping you?
Are you scared that they'll judge? Well, listen up, they have secrets too
Sharing secrets can bring people closer, sharing secrets can tell all the facts
Sharing secrets can show different views; sharing secrets can help you relax
So maybe if we all just grabbed a friend
And shared something we've been keeping inside
We'd all feel a little bit better having
Someone there with whom to confide

Wipe My Tears
by Jordyn Philbrook

I wiped the tears off my face, hoping all the pain would go away
I waited but nothing got better, I want to just melt away
Where did I go wrong?
But I know what I did wrong; I don't want to believe it
I don't want to admit it, if only I could go back in time
Would the world be better without me?
I wish I could share my feelings with someone
Will a friend help, a boy?
He could hold my hand from wiping my tears
He could use his hand to wipe them instead

Tiaryn
by Megan Gianniny

Sitting in the moonlight, staring at the sky
Frozen beauty, seen only by me
We turned the corner and my eyes lit up
As I saw its white shape outlined by the moon
The eyes, pale blue, seemed to see only me
Before rising on all fours and retreating into the trees
But the image of it stays, the powerful muscles
Hidden under warm, white fur, and the ears that seem to hear all
And the piercing eyes staring into my head
Tell me all I need to know about this wolf named Tiaryn

She
by Anna Carson

She's the one that quietly sits at the back of the classroom working hard
She's the one that never gets in trouble for misbehaving
She's the one that always tries to remain strong even when life isn't always great
She's the one that cries at night wishing to be happier
She's the one that never wants to be alone but she always is anyway
She's the one that doesn't want her life, but she deals
She's the one who cares for people that don't care for her
She's the one that wants to have more friends
She's the one who made this mistake once
That changed her life, maybe not forever
But for now she is still stuck, stuck in the world of hate
Not knowing where to go next or what to do
She's the one who's scared of change and that's what hurts her
She's the one who doesn't know who to turn to or who to trust
She's the one who cannot even trust herself
Where's the future headed, and what lies ahead for this girl?
The girl that is scared of change
The girl that has to deal with it everyday
And face the consequences of what she has done
And move on in order to enjoy life
This girl is the one to fear, for she is life

Hood Life
by Wilfredo Gonzalez, Jr.

The disease of the street is violence
Gang-bangers everywhere want to make you silenced
They want to make you deceased
And make your friends' tag, rest in peace
Little kids shot for no reason
And when you don't please them, they take your life like a precious gem
I see kids younger and poor on the streets, with nothing to kill their hunger
And I wonder what it would feel like to have nothing
But a button down shirt with only one button
It makes you think how you can have something, then in a blink it can be all gone
For every friend that said they had your back
Where they at, when you're running from 5-O, having an asthma attack?
Should you be like the rest and get shot in the chest
And have family and friends crying over your bed rest?

Their Eyes Shine Bright (Tribute To Hurricane Katrina Victims)
by Rebecca White

Their eyes shine bright like the stars in the sky
Filled with hope and promise for another day
Lives destroyed, homes gone
And yet, their eyes still shine bright
The cries of babies, the tears of men
The dreams lost but not yet forgotten
The hope of many, the sorrow of all
And yet, their eyes still shine bright
Like the stars in the sky, they glitter
But at the same time, they weep
They weep for the hurt, they weep for their loved ones
They weep for themselves, lives put on hold
Goals become second, and lives become first
Everyone comes together and comfort those they love
Hope is still alive in the air, and dreams are still in their hearts
A new beginning fresh in the midnight air
How do we know?
We know because their eyes still shine bright

Politically Incorrect
by Thomas Scanlan

I guess our President must be the missing link
Too bad we're like the Titanic and we're starting to sink
The vice is evil, medieval warfare
Our soldiers don't even get the rightful care
I bear my opinions on my arm
Too bad my arms can do no harm
But the question remains the same
Will Republicans or Democrats win the game?
When you think it's bad enough it only gets worse
Next thing you know half the enlistees are riding in a hearse
Too bad I'm running out of verse
I don't have all the facts
But it's not always terrorists pulling the attacks
We need oil, so get it, anyway you can
Fight for your country and go to Iran
Where there are children fighting at age eleven
I wonder if any of them will ever make it to heaven
I guess our President must be the missing link
Too bad we're like the Titanic and we're starting to sink

Love You Forever
by Kelvin Anderson

You are the one who is always there
The one who loves me till death is near
The one who I love for all my life
The one who I will love till the day I die
The one who loves me no matter what
The one I love with all my heart
The one who loves me even more
The one who is honest
The one that makes no promises
The one I have loved for almost all my life
The one I would give my life
Because she is the only girl that I ever loved
And the only one that keeps my heart beating and keeps me alive
I will always love you no matter what
And you know I love you with all my heart
And you are the best girlfriend I could ever have
Thank you for being there for me

Life Goes 'Round
by Nghi Truong

A circle begins with just a point
And goes around until it ends
The circle can represent
Life, family, and friends
The crooked edges are those times
You first begin to crawl and walk
You first learn how to potty
Or even when you first learn how to talk
As the circle continues on
The edges are sharpened by experiences
You become more independent through the years
You stand up from many difficult instances
But still, there may be some distortions and bulges
Of times when you're deeply hurt
Like when you lose your first true love
But remember, there's always people to give you comfort
Eventually, you reach the last few years
You're finally able to complete the circle
You lie down in a serene area
And everything around you is peaceful

Sherry
by Nicole Pinkham

Let's talk about a woman
A woman who created me
A woman whose life is full of love and pain
A woman whose wish is for her children to succeed
A woman whose pain never shows
A woman who keeps her feelings in to make sure no one around her gets hurt
A woman who wishes to wish upon a star and give me the world
A woman whose life is good but could be better
A woman who works to the fullest and never stops
A woman who makes me believe
A woman who stays in my heart and never leaves
My appreciation's to my mother

Rain
by Janie Rush

Rain falls in the fields
It sounds like footsteps running
From sinful angels

Goals
by Cindy Huynh

Goals are like money, you have to work hard to get them
Goals are as far as the moon, the only way to reach them is to make attempts
And learn from failures along the way
The road to making money starts with a job
But when they say, "No," I feel a slap on my face
Even though they say, "No," I make them regret their decision
To achieve my goals I must use tremendous tenacity
To get through all the obstacles in my path
I can feel the rubber gloves between my fingers
I can taste the sweet sensation of victory rolling down my tongue
I can smell the refreshing air of achievement
I can see the beauty of my success and my dream coming to life

Untitled
by Bruno Albuquerque

I don't know what to call this
A poem, a song, or a letter
But I do know that I want for us to be together
I used to live in reality
But since our eyes crossed I have been living in a fantasy
For this time that we are together it felt like a dream
But I prefer to dream, to be a dreamer ...
Than to be living in reality without you
Your dreamy eyes, they just won't say goodbye
That's why I think about you all the time
And I'm so happy, because I love someone that is mine

The Invisible Clock
by Beckett Dunning

Time is all around us, but is it real?
Time can't be touched or spoken to
Yet, we all speak of it, we make it real
We give it shape and form
It is true, we all need it
Yet, in a timeless world, how could we exist?
Could we live and walk and breathe?
We need time, and it needs us
But, can life exist without time?
This question exists, but it will never be answered
We will always use time
Until the day when our time is up

Angelina Waller

In addition to her literary talents,
Angelina is also musically gifted,
as she is able to play not only the piano,
but the mandolin and clarinet as well.
She has a medieval fascination,
which is evident in the decorating of her room,
and enjoys reading the works of several poets
including Edgar Allen Poe.
His influence can be seen
in Angelina's own dark masterpiece,
"Crows and Ravens"

Crows and Ravens
by Angelina Waller

Crows clothing a willow tree
Black feathers flow like silk in the breeze
A song of betrayal they sing
Either resting or flying
Ravens come, on the wing
Harkening sorrow as they sing
Now they blanket a walnut tree
A black sheet of misery
Crows and ravens of depression
Willows and walnuts of sadness
Now comes the rain, weeping for all

Emily Mergel

While we applaud her writing,
Emily tells us she is an actress at heart,
representing her school while in the eighth grade
at the state drama festival.
She is an artist and an avid reader
who still finds time to stay fit by running.
Her award winning poem, "So Clean and So Young"
is a compelling showcase of imagery,
which we found deserving of more than just 1ˢᵗ place
in the grade 8-9 division.
Therefore, we proudly present the work of Emily Mergel
Our 2006 Editor's Choice Award Winner.

So Clean and So Young
by Emily Mergel

Stagger down moonlit Willis Street
Patent leather spikes snagging in the crumbling asphalt
Collapse
Dizzy eyes are veiled by flickering lids
Head lolls back onto the silent pavement

Remember Christina
Suede and alabaster hands smooth a linen dress
Ice and ancient eyes glance away with somber sighs
Disapproval
Thin lips part

"Stop, little girl
Take time to smell the porch lights turning on
The rain dissolving paint on wooden houses
Breathe the way the would-be-junkies do
When getting blisters from holding hands too tight
Secrets too close
Love too dear"

Eyes flash
Eight thousand pear blossoms shower down upon a sorry face
Like kisses from thin lips, littering the moonlit pavement

Division IV
Grades 10-12

I Watched a Cherry Blossom Fall
by Jeff Goulet

I watched a cherry blossom fall, a cascade of soft petals
Its ethereal glance has that pale look, acceptance of fate
It knows that this fall will be the first, and the last
Admirers send it off, singing, "Sayonara, baby"
Shining its blushing smile one more time, before warm April breezes come
The angel of death breathes softly, and it falls

Changing Seasons
by Isaac Foss

As the sun rises over the rolling golden plains
A chill runs down my spine as the geese start singing
Feelings overwhelm me in a way I can't explain
The geese and ducks fly overhead all winging
The wind blowing against the hills makes waves
A deer in the distance makes his way to his bed
Leaves slowly flutter and fall to their wintry graves
Grass once green slowly turns into brown, dead
As the snow begins to descend from heaven it puts fall to sleep
Animals once invisible now exposed to all
The coyote and the fox move silently then leap
Everything slows down in the winter, almost to a crawl
Words cannot fully describe what I see
I hope you can understand what makes me, me

Standing Up
by Christopher Cotty

As jubilant as a coward
His fragile eyes, gray as pavement, are filled with rage and alertness
He slinks his way through the halls like a clown, juggling their insults
Processes like a typewriter, yet accepts it like a rejection letter
Bows his head like a palace guard
Noticing that he is not as invisible as he may want to be
Turns the dial of his lock like a roulette wheel
Hearing the enemy's shoes meeting the floor, he opens the locker
His enemy leans in with his ebony hand half in, like a stalker against a tree
The boy slams the locker shut like a cage
The coward is not a coward anymore

A Prayer For You
by Dominique Harris

I used to tell my granddaddy, "I love you this much"
I'd spread my arms as wide as I could and crack you a grin
But I didn't know I wouldn't ever see you again
'Cause you were more than a friend, you weren't useless
You never know how important something is
Until the moment comes and you lose it
I write lyrics for your spirit, 'cause I know you can hear it
This piece is from the heart, so your soul, I can't fear it
You were my dearest, but now you make the clouds lovely
If you were still living, I bet you would be proud of me
I've gained a nickname and try to do big things
Still in the streets, but a grandson you would claim
Dang, I miss you! I bite my lip and stay loyal
I know you're listening, so I love you and I'll pray for you
- Dedicated to Richard D. Todd

Exactly
by Ashleigh Day

Eighteen years of six foot tall, mid afternoon, baked playground
Sand colored hair, sporting left leg scar, right leg tat
Drag in, puff out
Baseball cap shabby, brim bent, edge frayed, dirt and grass stain covered fabric
Fistfight ending grounded
Drag in, puff out
Part time job, working fryers, grease spotted jeans, smelling week old chicken
Drag in, puff out
And that's exactly how he lives, or that's what he wants people to think
Nothing, of course, he ain't got nothing, but nothing can't go bad
Drag in, puff out
And he knows this river, mud caked feet step in rhythm, with the other
'Cause he's walking with another through yellow, gold, and green grass lined shore
Drag in, puff out
Fingers combing silk, dark brown hair
Smelling river breeze, chilling skin, exposed and tanned
Summer days with her, lips painted red, toenails dancing on sand
With his river angel
Drag in, puff out
And she's exactly why he lives

Sonnet
by Elizabeth Beatty

The sweetest fruit that ere did grace the Earth
Grows in the bright sunshine, what place?
A patch that when I see it fills me up with mirth
The berries and I are the perfect match
I hold the berry in my hand and see
How nature makes the most beauteous of fruit
The little seeds of strawberries to be
Add texture to the smooth, red skin, how cute!
Nothing compares to the fresh strawberry warmed from the sun
Its juicy nectar sweet, quenches my thirst
Setting my taste buds free
I wish the whole patch was for me to eat
But then I realize it's only March
'Tis not the season, and my lips grow parched

Empty Folder
by Scott Murphy

You are a blank empty folder
There is no content folded inside
The business men and powerbrokers
Feel no need to fill you with information
You are a bland, boring manila folder
You are lightweight due to the lack of substance filling your fold
When I look at you I feel nothing
Because you are an empty folder
Thin and plain, you hold no enticement

Invincible
by Stefanie Davis

Blue eyes full and bright
The sound of her voice, calm and collected, filled with endless love
She was the shepherd caring for her flock, healing hearts and drying eyes
But, too much agony has threatened those patient eyes and the heart is torn
She cowers behind a pessimistic shield and comes out scarcely
Only at times, not all times
Not even when she is needed most, by herself and others
Even a superhero can fall, fall to a villain
Her worst villain, her only villain, herself

Life
by Luke McMahon

Alone is the man at the wheel
If he were to slip off, he shall be sent back to the endless night
Who will be the unlikely human to free this man of his bonds?
A boy, young and innocent, the boy watches the man get older
As the old man looks down, he is looking at himself
The old man falls from the wheel, he is laid down in the arms of the boy
And as all life is expelled from the old man
The boy takes the wheel to continue the voyage of life

Beautiful Artist
by Monica Rosenberg

A poet is like an artist who sketches
With a sweep of the pencil creating an image
Meticulously, thought is conveyed on paper
Colored, painted on the canvas
A creation takes place
The sketchiness is enhanced by the artist
Through the mind till he's done
Pencils, pens, paints
Poetic words consume the artist's work with skill

In Heaven We'll Be
by Heather Stolz

The day has come when I move away
That day has come, nothing will be the same
Sadness comes and goes like the moon and sun
Sitting, watching the shimmering moon dancing on the lake
Reaching next to me for a gentle hand
But no one reaches back
In this moment a single tear falls
A hand reaches to brush the tear away
I look back at him, my love has come
I shut my eyes tight, hoping this moment will last forever
I feel a breeze; I open my eyes quickly, he is gone
This time I am not sad
I knew he did not want me to be
For he is waiting for our love to be
In Heaven waiting for me

The Irony of the English Language
by Eliza Coolidge

P
Ho
Netic

Love Hurts
by Jacquelyn Aulisio

Love is like a roller coaster ride
Remembering each and every scene by heart
Although it goes by fast on every side
With wild and mixed emotions from the start
Sometimes you want to laugh, or sit and cry
Live each second as if it never ends
Don't ever let a moment pass you by
Try to make it through the loops and bends
Don't give up too quick, just hold on tight
When it gets too bumpy, you might have to let go
Keep in mind it's best to just not fight
The end is coming close, you just don't know
Don't love too much, too easy, or too fast
Before you know it, it will be the past

The Soldier of the Dying Day
by Kyle Sullivan

Vision encumbered
By the constant spew of blackened earth and endless waves of annihilation
Shrills of misery just shy of earshot
Splinters of white protrude out of green and gray
Harshly serrated and partly decayed
Beasts beckon for flame, super-heated sea of rain
The flesh rives and burns, mutilation and human emotion
So much easier than creation
A green figure, a soldier of fortune, rises to meet his fate
Projectiles soar, nestle in the flesh
Falling down, the body crumples and turns
Life is leaving him in a most peculiar way
The soldier of the dying day

The Man Inside the Moon
by Eugene Emmanuel Dixon, Jr.

There's a man inside the moon! Do you know him? Not I
I hear he's friends with Atlas, the one who holds the sky
His face seems kind and warm as he rises each new day
But today he does not greet me, though the sky is not gray
They say that he will return for his reunion with Sol
They say that they've been friends the longest, since before the days of old

Death
by Jack Retterson

Death is dark
We remember the light
Only black backgrounds
Our closed eyes
To hear no one in the distance
Our body decays in our tomb
Then we become ash
Death is dark
Do you know if there is an afterlife?
You have to die to find out
But you don't believe it's true
But God talks to you
Death is dark

Secrets
by Felicia Bonney

She touched his face with her icy cold fingertips
He could see her frigid breath
Began crying clear crystal tears
She whispered secrets into his ears
She said things she could only say
Talking of a beautiful disaster
He laid on his bed and screamed
Falling through the cracks in his mind
She would tell him to wait until the sallow sun went down
When she would come back
The only thing was, she would never be back

Sonnet
by Liana Roach

Revenge for twenty years, the need consumed
Vendettas born behind the silv'ry mask
Of one, long hidden under tree and moon
Heart cold to all but his forbidden task
The task he executed perfectly
Until one cold, dark night, he found the one
He healed her terror, helped to set her free
And asked to see her ere his task was done
The bond between them grew to something more
One dance was all they e'er would get to share
His death came swift; she had no time to mourn
His dying breath whispered his love and care
She finished his task, changed the world forever
With freedom found that night in sweet November

Whispers
by Rachel Miller

Whispers of sweet nothings, escape from the threads
Your gaunt, blue pullover, with years of fighting under its belt
Those threads gave me worries, you moved in way too fast
I'm not good at hiding; I tried to escape, getting caught in your web
Like a mere fly, I was under your black widow spell
We had dramatic endings, Shakespearean twists
You die like Romeo; I lie with your hoodie, like Juliet
I never wanted you to love me

Shalom
by Eric Silva

I see this page, a blank canvas
Every word, a stroke of the brush
I see this page, a blank canvas
Though nervous, I try not to rush
For my words may never leave these walls
I won't get out alive
Though I may never leave these walls, this canvas may survive
My painting's done, and just in time
I say to you, "Shalom"
For I must go outside these walls, outside these walls, alone

Even When You've Gone Away
by Kathryn Roy

Even when you've gone away
In my heart you'll always stay
Your smile is in the morning sun
The wind holds your voice filled with fun
I'll hear your laugh in caverns so deep
Memories of you, I'll cherish and keep
I've watched you struggle with this disease so vain
And watched you smile through the pain
And all this time my only hope
Was just to get to hold you close
And say, "I love you," one last time
Until we meet in eternity divine

Rain
by Ashleigh Nicholson

Exploding anger
Descending ferociously
I taste refreshment

Sailing
by Julia Saltanovich

The golden sun shines on the crystal lake
My sailboat sparkles and shines like a jewel
The wind decides what direction to take
A perfect summer day, not hot, nor cool
So far away from harsh reality
A soothing gust of wind runs through my hair
A world of calmness and serenity
In this moment, I don't have a care
The boat cuts through the water like a blade
The wind is at our backs and blowing strong
There is nothing in the world I'd trade
For this day, on the water I belong
A day aboard a sailboat sets you free
I learned this lesson sailing on the sea

In Loving Memory
by Lydia Nelson

Sadness is in my soul; I'm condemned to living life in hell
Misery, I've had my share, justice isn't pain, love shouldn't be quilted shame
Heartache, so many tears in a corner of lies, wrapped up by pretty bows I've tied
Hate calibrates, retaliates, my fear
Serenity, please give me peace, set my bleeding heart to ease
Let me seize to the truth, I love every one of you
Too soon the suffering I take when I can stand from the past
There's another blast of misery, I shed a million tears of loss
A lesson I wish I was never taught
In my memory I'll see you standing there
The way you did, the way you should
The way I always knew you could
- In memory of Mouse, Alan, and Kendan

I'm a Living Ghost
by Darcie L. Kingeekuk

So many years I've been hurt, got hit into the dirt
I've been in many fights because I know my rights
I feel like it's just me, I always cry but I don't know why
Every day I pray so hard to have a better life, and cry myself to sleep
The pain hurts in my heart, that it is so deep
All the pain that wants to be released, but something holds on to it too tight
Nobody asks me if I am all right
I have many bruises inside my heart, but it isn't torn apart
Some part of me is missing, and my life is depressing
This is very unfair, and I wish you would care
People hating on me, obviously
I feel like no one can see me
I'm a living ghost and being hated most
When I'm gone, I am haunting you first, because you are my worst

Corruption
by Kimberly Kurzendoerfer

The hidden beauty
Trapped inside a leafy shell of the spawning bud
The innocence of the blooming bud speaks only of its coming life
Now in full bloom, a deep blood-red tells of what it's silently witnessed
And it wilts alone, petals floating softly to the ground
Silent for always

Other People and You
by Rachel Frederickson

Some people care what other people think, but not you
Some people see that as an admirable quality, but not me
If you don't care what others think, will you care when I say
"Please don't wear surf shorts and your shirt unbuttoned to my father's funeral"
Will you stop putting your needs in front of those people
Who need your comfort and support?
Will you start caring what other people think?

Fate
by Matthew Mullaney

Rising up for the mountain peaks
The sun shines
Gleaming down over the ground that its light seeks
As it peers through the clouds in impenetrable lines
As it rises, the Earth makes its shift
We go from night to day in a blink
Never fully catching our breath as we drift
Trying to find our own human link
We can only guess where the day will lead our lives
We can only wonder what the day will bestow
Our time may be revealed as the sun arrives
But what will the future show?

Sarah Adams

Now in the eleventh grade,
Sarah is a whirlwind of activity.
Reading, writing, dancing,
horseback riding, and Tae Kwon Do
are some of her favorite pastimes.
Oh, we almost forgot, she's also learning
to play the piano and speak Japanese,
all challenging yet enjoyable aspects
of Sarah's well-rounded home school regimen.
She tells us her dream is to visit Ireland.
If past and present accomplishments are any indication,
we're sure she'll have a wonderful trip.

Farewell To Childhood
by Sarah Adams

In the nursery down the hall
Thick silence fills the air
The toys stand ready on the shelves
But no young boy is there
He has his briefcase, suit and tie
He has no use for things
Like dragon tales and paper hats
And dust of pixie's wings
The rocking-horse grows dusty
Look closer and you'll trace
A slow parade of ashen tears
Upon his oaken face
He loved that little boy the best
And wonders how he'll fare
When child-like innocence is lost
Replaced with work and care
And so the world cheers its new man
While tears fill wooden eyes
For where the world sees triumph
The rocking-horse, demise

Eric Rostvedt

Eric was a senior in high school
when he penned this very poignant and personal account
of the crucifixion.
A deeply rooted young man,
Eric enjoys reading and writing.
His apt descriptions
of the parts played
by hope, love, and mercy
in the ultimate sacrifice,
do justice to the subject matter of his work
and we congratulate him on a wonderful poem.
Thank-you Eric.

The Price of Love
by Eric Rostvedt

The darkness loomed on such a day
When Faith held her tongue
Unrighteous men cowered away
When on the cross He hung
Their King, their Friend, was dying there
His burdened eyes looked down
Yet, while He hung, He said a prayer
And wore His crimson crown
The thorns, they mocked His royalty
Innocence hammered the nails
The sinners proclaimed disloyalty
And darkness said, "Hope fails!"
It was true, Hope had to hide
Her tears stained the light
But Love, she shone! She turned the tide!
For mercy, Love would fight
Nail-pierced hands raised the sword
The King, with His final breath
Struck down the Enemy, and the Lord
For wretched us, chose death

Index

of

Authors

Index of Authors

Index of Authors

Index of Authors

Stahl, Colin 162
Staras, Sabrina 124
Stark, Nathan 79
Staton, Jeffrey 63
Steen, Kimberly 124
Steffey, Bambi 139
Stolz, Heather 207
Strickland, Kimmy 78
Sullivan, Kyle 208
Supple, Evan 94
Szpyrka, Amber 82

T

Taborda, Karen 174
Talbot, Christopher 181
Tejada, Ruth 189
Theroux, Evan 145
Thomas, Ethan 169
Thompson, Aubrey 27
Tippenhauer, Nathan 46
Towne, Katie 47
Towne, Steven 77
Tracy, Zach 4
Trainor, Ryan 125
Tranthem, Taylor 26
Trask, Wesley 74
Truong, Nghi 195
Tucker, Benjamin 159
Tyree, Mariah 44

U

Ullom, Jacob 115

V

Vasselin, Christine 105
Vaught, McKenzie 13
Vespa, Shauna 85
Vishwanath, Anjali 14
von Borstel, Ashley 43

W

Waller, Angelina 199
Wang, Emma 19
Wang, Jiayuan 167
Wasson, Alexandria 132
Waszak, Andrew 103
Wathen, Kendall 4
Watts, Shelby 16
Weber, Griff 33
Weithofer, Gabriella 39
West, Bethany 13
Whiles, Zachary 23
White, Bobby 84
White, Rebecca 194
Wilding, Hope 25
Wilding, Lily 24
Wilkinson, Tess 185
Wilson, Rachel 126
Wise, Olivia 78
Witt, Morgan 37
Wolf, Whitney 163
Wolsfelt, Hanna 186
Wood, Terrelle 14
Woodrum, Brittney 112
Worthington, Quinn 162

Y

Yoder, Kate 81
Yong, Daniel 100
Young, Lindsey 37

Z

Zhang, Thompson 81

Excellence
Price List

Initial Copy.................................32.95

Additional Copies........................ 24.00

*Please Enclose $6 Shipping/Handling Each Order

Check or Money Order Payable to:

The America Library of Poetry
P.O. Box 978
Houlton, Maine 04730

Must specify book title and author

Please Allow 21 Days For Delivery

THE AMERICA
LIBRARY OF POETRY

www.libraryofpoetry.com
Email: generalinquiries@libraryofpoetry.com

Poetry On the Web

See Your Poetry Online!

This is a special honor reserved exclusively for our published poets.

Now that your work has been forever set in print,
why not share it with the world at www.libraryofpoetry.com

At the America Library of Poetry,
our goal is to showcase quality writing in such a way as to inspire
others to broaden their literary horizons,
and we can think of no better way to reach people around the world
than by featuring poetic offerings like yours on our global website.

Since we already have your poem in its published format,
all you need to do is copy the information from the form below on
a separate sheet of paper, and return it with a $6 posting fee.
This will allow us to display your poetry
on the internet for one full year.

Author's Name _____

Poem Title _____

Book Title _____ *Excellence* _____

Mailing Address _____

City _____ State _____ Zip Code _____

Check or Money Order in the amount of $6 payable to:
The America Library of Poetry
P.O. Box 978
Houlton, Maine 04730